Brian McGowan

Develop your Inner Coach

Selling

All the skills you need to become your own Mental Coach and see your sales and confidence grow

ISBN-13: 978-1497324190

.

Dedication

To every unsung salesperson out there travelling the miles up and down the country, without whom industry and commerce would grind to halt. You deserve every success your talent and dedication brings and it's my pleasure to be part of it.

TABLE OF CONTENTS

Introduction

Introduction

When you think about it, what makes a Professional Sales person?

Is it their:

- Sales Skills?

- Planning Skills?

- Communication Skills?

- Product and Industry Knowledge?

- Confidence?

- Experience?

- All of the above?

So then the next question is - do you have them?

If you're reading this, I guess the answer to the above is yes and you're probably looking for ways to add to your skills and gain an advantage over your competitors. Correct?

OK, so now let me ask the same question of another type of Professional.

What makes a Top Professional Sports Person? Let's say a top Golfer.

It could be that their:

- Swing is perfect and consistent.

- They're an excellent ball striker – true and straight.

- Their putting is top drawer.

- They're excellent at Course Management.

- They're physically fit for the challenge.

Yet, if all the above is true (which it is) - even the *greatest* players in the world only win 10 – 20% of the time they play. Nobody wins all the time!

So what keeps them going?

How can someone who only wins 20% of the time, such as Tiger Woods – be called the greatest? Surely, if he's the best at all of the categories mentioned before, he'd win every time?

Interesting thought isn't it?

There's an old saying in golf frequently used when a player is in a slump – "You don't become a bad player overnight". Meaning the skills you've honed over the years don't just suddenly evaporate.

Yet Tiger almost disappeared off the world rankings "overnight" when he went through his off course personal problems a few years back and it's *that* situation that gives us a clue to the **real nature** of winners.

Yes, you need the skills. Of course you need to know what you're doing. But the real difference between winners and also-rans is not their skill or knowledge but how they **THINK**!

You can put a cigarette paper between the golfing skills of most top Pro's on the tour – they're all *that good*. What makes the difference week in and week out is how they **think** and how they **feel** when they are playing.

It only takes 1 shot less than your opponent to win a golf tournament.

One goal more than the other team to win a match.

$1/10,000^{th}$ of a second quicker than the field to win the 100 meters final!

It's the smallest of margins that separates winning and losing amongst professionals. Meaning it's the small things that matter, the hidden little gems that give the winners the edge over their competition.

That's why Tiger plummeted down the world rankings, his mind wasn't in a fit state to play never mind win! Yet as I write this, he's now back to his best and sitting on top of the world rankings once again. The king is back!

Developing your *Inner Sales Coach* is about fine tuning the mental skills that will give you that same advantage. A set of mental skills that will see off your competition and help you climb to the top of your company or industry rankings.

This is not a book about how to present features and benefits when selling – you should already know how to do that and if you don't – there are plenty of great sources of learning out there that cover such selling skills. This is about giving you the **performance edge**, the mental keys to unlock your true sales potential if and I mean *if*, you are prepared to open your mind and take on board tried and tested mental game principles developed over years in the sports arena.

It's these skills that separate true champions from average players. These are the inner skills that keep you focussed, help you perform when the pressure is on and give you control over the greatest asset that you have - **Your Mind**.

So, if by learning these skills you end up being miles ahead of the competition in your industry – great – enjoy it. But remember, just like professional sportsmen and women all over the globe, all you need is to be *just* in front when it matters most to win the order and that's down to how you think and perform throughout the sales process.

Developing your Inner Sales Coach looks at the **6 key mental skills** professional sportsmen and women use to give them the edge so you can apply them in your day to day selling activities.

I know this works, my background is Sales and Marketing. I've sold products and services, managed Sales Teams and I've been training Sales Forces throughout the UK for many years on all the traditional basic and advanced sales & negotiation skills that you'll be familiar with. Then everything changed a few years back when I qualified in Sports Psychology. Then it all made sense. If you don't think right – you don't perform to the best of your ability, regardless of your knowledge and skill level.

The Sports arena has spent millions of dollars and decades of research getting to the bottom of this fact and you are about to benefit from all that work.

In professional sports the competition is getting tougher and it's getting harder and harder to reach the top. For every golfer, tennis player or footballer you see on television there are literally tens of thousands - playing, striving desperately to make it to the top - that we never hear of and the sad thing is, many of them may be just as talented as those familiar names we know and love; McIlroy, Woods, Murray, Federer, Ronaldo, Rooney – yet they never make it.

Could it just be luck?

Perhaps, occasionally. But it's more likely down to being mentally tough and dedicated; having the will to go the extra mile to learn something, develop a skill or hone a talent - that's what separates the top Pro's from the rest. It's a **Mental Attitude**.

Winners have an inner determination to be all they can be. That's what makes them stand out. That's why they have the skills, the success and all the rewards that follow.

So congratulations on taking a massive step forward by being willing to develop your Inner Sales Coach – becoming your own mental game expert.

The most important component in any sale is you. ***People buy people first.*** If you are professional, calm, in control and focussed – that will come across to your customers and prospects. When you think right – you perform right and in the sales arena there's normally no prize for coming second – no silver or bronze. You either win the order or you don't! So any advantage you can gain over the competition is worth having.

So how should you use this book?

If you must, read it right through from start to finish but please promise yourself that you will work on each of the skills until they become habit.

That means practice and dedication, not one quick pass.

So return to each section and work at it until the mental skill described within is embedded. Each mental skill may take weeks or longer to master but every step along the way you will be improving, developing and stretching out in front of the competition.

Remember, anything worth having is worth fighting for. You owe it to yourself to be the best you can be and in return attain the rewards you desire.

Enjoy the Journey. Embrace the Success.

Brian McGowan

Mental Skill Number 1:

Attitude and Self-Talk

Mental Skill Number 1:
Attitude and Self-Talk

Ok let me be upfront here – I'm not going to lecture you on staying positive – being all happy-clappy and keeping your chin up when the going gets tough. That's not what *I* mean by attitude. If it were that easy everyone would be doing it. Agreed?

So I need to start by giving out some tough love.

Like it or not, you are a creature of habit. Psychologists reckon that 90% of what you get up to day to day is done on automatic pilot; you get out of bed the same way, brush your teeth the same way, put on your trousers – same leg first, sit in the car resting your left leg in the same position.

You have your favourite haunt for coffee, begin your sales calls the same way, have the same manner on the telephone etc. etc.

In a nutshell, over the years, you have developed a repertoire of well-honed habits that enshroud your job, your personal life and every aspect of life you partake of; sports, hobbies, study, faith and so on - throughout all of them - you will find you have habitual behaviours taking place.

Just think about that for a moment.

Day to day you perform habitual "rituals" without thinking about it.

Now if those "rituals" are good, beneficial to you, your health and your wealth - fantastic.

However, many of those habitual acts are actually bad for you. You no longer **THINK** – you just do things and those things can become unintentional roadblocks to your personal growth and success without you even noticing - because they're habits!

Now add into this mix - our self-talk - our constant internal dialog and we're in danger of producing a recipe for disaster!

We "say" thousands of things to ourselves every day and most (80% or so) are negative in nature.

I shouldn't have said that…. That buyer doesn't like me…. He's going to hate the terms and conditions…. We're way out on price…. Bloody Traffic…. Why doesn't she return my call?…. Here we go, another sales meeting, bashing figures…. I can never plan my week…. I'm always late.

Sound familiar?

Well, this has to stop.

Being successful is hard enough without you helping the opposition by bringing yourself down! And yes, you know you do it even if not to the extremes outlined above.

One of the few things in life we have direct and absolute control over is our thoughts. And that's what self-talk is - our thoughts.

The second you hear that internal voice saying something negative about yourself, the situation you are in or how the customer may react . . . **STOP**! Challenge it.

If *you* think you're expensive, what do you think the customer is going to sense when the price is discussed?

Don't you think Nadal or Murray "smells blood" when their opponent looks worried? Of course they do and the buyer sitting opposite you is a trained professional too or an astute business owner who knows how to wheel and deal.

Self-talk is where it all begins and ends.

If you think you'll lose – you will. If you focus on the price being too high or the features that are weaker than your competitors', they will manifest themselves in the sales call as sure as eggs are eggs.

If I may paraphrase, Henry Ford once said, "Whether you think you can or you think you can't, you're right."

Everything we do begins with a thought.

Do you think an Olympian can win gold harbouring doubts about their ability? No chance. Self-belief is paramount and it begins with your own self-talk - your thoughts - so stop beating yourself up!

It's a fact we say things to ourselves that we'd punch someone for if they said it to our face. I know. I'm a golfer and in the past I've called myself every offensive name under the sun when I've played a bad shot, totally ignorant of what it was doing to me.

Apart from the fact I wouldn't accept being called that from another human being walking the planet, I had no idea back then that I was programming my subconscious to believe what I was saying and the more I did it, I was creating a self-fulfilling prophesy - I was becoming the *no good, awful player* I was describing myself as on the course. (*Italicised* words sanitised for the feint hearted!)

Your subconscious doesn't care what it's programmed with. It simply records and remembers, while cleverly filing and categorising things for instant recall - normally at the most inappropriate and inopportune times.

Let me demonstrate this.

Have you ever been driving along in the car when a song comes on the radio and suddenly - **BANG** - you're back in time, memories flooding in, emotions running riot and your mood either lifts or deteriorates depending on what memories the song brings to mind? Sound familiar? It's happened to us all.

As you were happily rolling along, you didn't ask for the intrusion to happen, for your state of mind to change - it just did. Your subconscious flooded your brain with thoughts, emotions and feelings you didn't ask for (good or bad). And the fact is, whenever that song plays you'll feel the same way every time.

But why?

The answer is because your subconscious mind was programmed by you to react this way - albeit unintentionally.

At the time the song was in vogue, you were talking to yourself as you usually do - all that "self-talk"- but now fuelled with emotion about the break up or fantastic romance on holiday. Good or bad, it doesn't matter - your subconscious mind recorded it all and now when the song is played, even years apart, you immediately revert to the same emotional state, totally involuntary.

Now, having gone through that example and probably having experienced it yourself, would you accept that the thoughts you have influence your feelings? Yes? Of course they do.

What you are thinking dictates your mood.

Then you will also accept that how you feel affects your behaviour too. If you feel good you're up for it and throw yourself headlong into what you're doing and enjoy it but if you feel down, you couldn't care less and perhaps attempt things half-heartedly.

What you think (self-talk) changes how you feel. How you feel affects your behaviour and the last bit of the equation is also simple to understand - your behaviour directly influences your results.

What you do or don't do brings you success in life or failures and frustrations.

Let me repeat Henry Ford's words, "Whether you think you can or you think you can't, you're right."

Your **thoughts** dictate your **results** - they are directly connected and remember, for most of the human race, the vast majority of all that self-talk is negative! That's why Ford's words are so powerful.

So from now on - make a stand. Catch your negative self-talk before it makes you under-perform. The power is in your own hands. What you say to yourself is up to you and no one else.

When you hear yourself saying, "I can't", change it to "why not?"

Change he won't, to he will!

Change too expensive, to value for money.

Change I'm afraid, to what's the worst that can happen?

It's all down to you.

At the end of the book you'll find some practical ideas to help you overcome typical selling issues such as Getting Appointments and Handling Objections - two classic areas that cause salespeople problems on a daily basis. Once you're on top of these, you won't find so many negative thoughts entering your mind, allowing you to be in control at all times and remain confident and focused.

Successes

However, despite any negative self-talk you may have indulged in during your sales career to date, there will have been successes in there too, I'm sure of that!

So I'd like you to take a moment and think back over your career to a time when you were successful. Don't rush it, take your time and reflect fully on any success you've had to date.

Perhaps it was a BIG sale against all the odds? A difficult situation you turned around? Your first ever sale? Being promoted?

Whatever the successes were, just take a moment and let the memories come back to you . . . .

Now as you read this passage, keep the memory there . . . Just allow the feelings of success to sink in.

Take notice of how you feel when recalling this memory.

Is your heart "lighter"? Do you feel happy? Do you sense a smile on your face? Perhaps your chest is held high, proud and confident?

Once again, take the time to let the memory and feelings sink in. Look away from the page and repeat the exercise, let the feelings take effect, see and feel what success - **your success** - is like.

Doesn't it feel good?

And it's your own memory, your own success.

So wouldn't it be great to tap into this and feel this way more often?

Well, thankfully you can and the good news is that it's down to you to decide.

In Psychology, there is a concept called **Premature Cognitive Commitment**. What this means is that we operate out of automatic, habitual behaviours that we've developed by learning and growing.

Another way of saying this is to use the phrase "**Learned Behaviour**". As human beings, what we are is a result of our life experiences and our reactions to them - and in this respect we're no different to any other species that inhabit this earth.

You may well know the story of Pavlov's Dogs. (Ivan Pavlov was a Russian Behavioural Scientist, just in case you didn't know!) What Pavlov did was to ring a bell and at the same time he fed a pack of dogs. This process, he repeated over and over. Then, one day, he just rang the bell - and guess what? The dogs salivated and began prancing around in anticipation of the food.

Pavlov deduced his theory of stimulus-response from this experiment. To you and I the dogs were exhibiting learned behaviour - the bell meant food.

When you recalled the time you were successful, you were exhibiting the same automatic reactions as Pavlov's dogs. Thinking of your success made you feel good. Feel strong. Feel powerful and in control.

Yet all too often in sales, the opposite learned behaviour takes over. The **negative**.

We think that lifting the phone to make an appointment will result in a refusal and when it happens, we unwittingly programme our subconscious with "see told you" and build up a resistance to doing the very things we need to do, in order to be successful.

Remember, Professional Golfers - which in case you haven't realised is my sport of choice - only win a fraction of the time; but does that stop them from entering tournaments?

"Oh no point, chances are I won't win! I only win one in five outings!"

It would be incredulous to hear a professional sportsperson say that wouldn't it?

These guys don't focus on the negative. They look towards what they *can* do to aid success. If that means playing more tournaments and travelling around the globe to ensure they collect enough points to be in the Ryder Cup Team - they do it.

In sales, if that means acknowledging you need to make 20 phone calls to get through to 5 people of whom 1 will see you - you do it – because that's what brings you success.

Let me back this up with another example. Have you ever driven a new car? Did it feel good? Smell great? Wonderful isn't it?

Now think of what happened when you took it down the motorway or freeway when it was still new to you. Was your beautiful new car unique and singularly yours or did you notice a few - or more than a few - similar models on the road?

What you were experiencing was a reaction to you being transfixed, focussed on your shiny new vehicle.

Your mind automatically brought to your attention, pointed out, attracted to you the thing you were obsessed with - your car.

But not just the one you were in!

Oh, no! Your subconscious went into overdrive and made you see "your car" everywhere. The normal day to day filtering that your mind uses to ignore things that are not relevant, suddenly went into reverse and brought to your attention the thing you were focussed on.

This feature of the brain is called the Reticular Activator System or RAS for short. Our mind will "see" what we focus on and make it known to us.

Normally, part of our subconscious mind's function is to filter out stuff we don't need. For example, if I ask you to feel your shoe or sock on your right foot - that feeling has always been there but your subconscious filters it out so you are not overloaded with irrelevant data.

However, the subconscious can also focus on things we obsess with and bring to our conscious mind - the thinking, logical, rational part of our brain - information that helps us attain what we're thinking about, hence noticing cars that are the same as your new one.

But you must be aware; this function of the mind is not selective.

Focus on positive ideas and outcomes that you're excited about and the RAS will help you find them but focus on negative outcomes and worries and guess what - the RAS will work in that instance too and all too often you'll get what you are thinking about.

Remember you're fighting programming here. 80% of your self-talk is negative. So because self-talk is nothing more than thoughts, your RAS will help you achieve what you think about and obsess over - another great reason to start thinking and talking to yourself in a positive manner!

In a moment I'll come back to the RAS and give you a powerful technique that activates the success seeking part of your mind so you can fully engage with it to aid your success but first I'd like to return to the title of this chapter, Attitude and Self-Talk.

Attitude is all about having the right **Mind-Set** for the situation you are in. Let me repeat that if I may.

Attitude is all about having the right Mind-Set for the situation you are in.

Think about it, every sales call you face day to day is different - just as to a golfer each course they play, is different.

Every customer or prospect you meet is different. And to a golfer the tournament's opponents may be different.

Each sales call may require different sales skills (Objection Handling, Selling the Benefits, Probing & Questioning techniques or Presenting a Proposal) depending on what stage the sale is at.

And to golfers, they may use different clubs - play more bunker shots one round over another – They may have to fade the ball or draw the ball or play flop shots in and around the green - all depending on the type of course or weather conditions they're facing.

The point is, in both situations - in sales and in sport - there are similarities each time and differences each time. But to be successful *you* need to be able to handle the situation, play the shot, when it's called for.

Now if you struggle with a sales skill, let's say getting appointments - just like the golfer who struggles with putting - you need to practice that skill. And here again it's all about mind-set.

I see people in driving ranges up and down the country booming drives 250 yards into the distance - impressive - but it's a skill they are good at - they can do it! So why spend an hour on this when they will 3 putt half a dozen greens on Saturday during the monthly medal? Sure it's more fun - doing what you're good at - but does that honestly make you better?

How about working on eliminating the weaknesses? That's what champions do. They work to improve their whole game.

How about you in sales? What do you work on improving?

You cannot be totally confident in your sales abilities if you have a weakness.

For example, I have worked with sales people who have "Price Fright" - they dread the price objection coming up.

But here's the issue - the problem lies with them not the customer!

It's the customer's job to question the price, they want ensure they're getting the best deal. But if the salesperson thinks he or she is overpriced and not value for money - they will live in mortal fear of the objection arising. Does that make sense?

The sales person is putting pressure on themselves - it's not the customer who's creating the pressure!

Again it's like a golfer dreading going into bunkers or a darts player needing to hit the bull - which he can never do!!

It's not rocket science - if you have a weakness, practice to improve it.

Now as this is about your mental skills, I'll come back to where I started.

Our self-talk is responsible for most of the negative thoughts we experience each and every day. But it's within our direct control to halt them as soon as they arise.

Do not focus on worries and negative thoughts. If you do they will fulfil themselves - that's the function of the reticular activator system and you are engaging it unknowingly.

If you've ever played golf, what happened when you stood on the tee and thought "hope I don't top this drive" or "I hope this doesn't go in the water" Well?

Your body manifests your thoughts - you went in the water. In selling, your customers sense this - it's called **projection**. So take control.

If a salesperson is frightened of their prices they need to regain confidence - they need to look into *why* they are the price they are:

Are their products better quality?

Do they include additional components such as warranty, service etc. that competitors don't?

They need to rationalise the price in their own minds and be confident. Perhaps the better car and higher basic salary than the competition provide, also has something to do with the product prices being higher - just a thought!

Whatever area requires attention in your sales armoury, in your sales skills, acknowledge it and give it some attention. Read up on it, ask your Sales Manager about it, get training or coaching on it and practice it; so you are confident and in total control when in front of your customers.

As I've said, **Attitude** is all about having the right **Mind-Set** for the situation you are in. So do what you can to feel confident and in control when selling.

So once more, take a moment and think back over your career to a time when you had a good successful outcome.

Let the memory come back to you . . . .

Again, keep it there . . . and take notice of your feelings.

The feelings you are sensing are what you want to have when you sell, when you perform your chosen career - your skill.

When you feel like this you have the right Attitude to tackle anything. You're in the right frame of mind!

Think like this before every sales call you make from now on in.

Be in the right state of mind to win.

Activate the RAS to help you achieve what you want

When you do the above exercise, when you are thinking like this, recalling memories, seeing, feeling and perhaps hearing what went on - you are visualising and talking to yourself (self-talk) because the two go hand in hand - pictures and dialog.

But what you are really doing is practicing what is called **Visualisation** or **Mental Imagery** and it's a skill Professional Sports men and women know all about and it's one that can **greatly influence** your sales success because it automatically gets you focussed on what you want - as you're virtually dreaming about it, focussing on it, even obsessing about it - if the subject of your thought raises enough passion within you.

So how can you adapt this to Selling?

This technique of Visualisation and Mental Imagery can be used in various ways to aid your sales game:

You can use it to visualise success: Many sportspeople "see" themselves achieving their goals on a regular basis, performing skills at a high level and seeing their desired performance outcomes.

The reason they do this is because the subconscious mind does not differentiate between what's imagined and what's real.

Think about when you last had a real bad nightmare - you wakened up with a jump, heart pounding and perhaps soaked in sweat. But was someone chasing you? Did someone have a knife standing over you? No! But your body was reacting as though it was real. Your mind didn't say "Hey chill out bud, this is only a dream" - it didn't know and so sent real fight - flight signals to your body.

You can use this to your benefit. As I said, your subconscious mind does not differentiate between what's imagined and what's real. So rehearse enough mentally, and your mind will believe just like professional sportspeople do.

You can use Visualisation and Mental Imagery to motivate yourself: Before or during a day's selling, calling up images of your goals for that day or of a past success or future call where you visualise it all going well – this can act as a positive motivator. It can remind you of your objectives, which can result in increased focus during your day or when you're planning and preparing.

Mentally focussing on: why you are doing what you're doing is a powerful stimulant.

Do you want to be top salesperson in the company? Perhaps win that weekend away for two? Or do you have visions way beyond what you're currently doing and see this as a stepping stone to greater things - perhaps Sales Manager, Director or President?

Mental Imagery and Visualisation work wonders when combined with goals - a topic we'll look at in the next chapter.

You can use Mental Imagery and Visualisation to perfect skills: Mental Imagery is often used to aid the learning and refinement of skills.

The best sportspeople "see" and "feel" themselves performing perfectly during competition. They go over in their mind's eye their routines, their actions, their techniques on a regular basis - they see themselves performing well and to their fullest ability.

It's no coincidence those at the top of any sport *see* themselves as winners.

Once again, consider how this can be used in a Sales context - the more you see yourself presenting, handling objections and closing sales - the more your mind will accept this as the "norm" for you and you will act automatically in ways that move you closer to your goals and success.

You can use Mental Imagery to familiarise yourself - with all kinds of things, such as an up and coming presentation, seeing how you will deliver it, creating a game plan, familiarise yourself with what you will do in a sales call or a refocusing plan - how do you get back on track should things go wrong?

There are many applications where mental imagery can help you become familiar with all aspects of your sales process.

So how do you Apply Mental Imagery?

In describing how he employs mental images to enhance his performance, Jack Nicklaus once wrote:

"I never hit a shot, even in practice, without having a sharp in-focus picture of it in my head. It's like a colour movie. First, I "see" the ball where I want it to finish, nice and white and sitting up high on the bright green grass. Then the scene quickly changes, and I "see" the ball going there: its path, trajectory, and shape, even its behaviour on landing. Then there's a sort of fade-out, and the next scene shows me making the kind of swing that will turn the previous images into reality - only at the end of this short private Hollywood spectacular do I select a club and step up to the ball." [1]

The world's greatest living golfer - advocating mental imagery.

However, having this skill on tap comes only through practice - it doesn't become second nature overnight. If you want to perfect and use mental imagery to your fullest advantage you can start by doing two things:

When you're planning and preparing your call, first imagine it happening as perfectly and precisely as possible. See, feel, and experience yourself moving through the sales process in your mind as you would like it to actually happen.

Knowing what your objective is on each call is imperative; is it a prospecting cold call? A fact find? Are you presenting a proposal or closing the deal? Make sure you rehearse and visualise what is to happen on the call, so your subconscious will lead you in the right direction.

When in with Customers, while in reception before the sales call starts, mentally recall your game plan, sales skills pertinent to the objectives for that call, focus skills, reactions or feelings that you want to carry into the call.

It all helps re-enforce your confidence, focus and ability *and* remember, customers need to have confidence in you - if they don't - they won't buy.

Who wants to deal with someone they don't feel confident in? Would you? So you need to start the process by re-enforcing your own self-confidence before you meet them.

However, to become highly proficient in the use of visualisation and mental imagery, you have to use it every day, on your way to calls, during calls, after the call and in the evenings before sleeping.

This is what professional sportsmen and women do.

To be the best they eat, sleep and drink their sport and most of the time it's all going on in their minds.

Another way of looking at this is Daydreaming.

How many times a day does your mind wander to the weekend or your next round of golf or up and coming holiday?

You're already using mental imagery when this happens - all I'm suggesting is that you become your own movie director and get a bit of cohesion and structure to what you are already capable of doing and let it help your sales success.

Reflections on Mental Skill Number 1:

Set yourself goals and objectives for implementing the use of Positive Self-Talk and Mental Imagery to get a great attitude going.

List them here:

Mental Skill Number 2:

Self-Motivation

Mental Skill Number 2:
Self-Motivation

The sales arena is a strange one when it comes to motivation. It relies heavily on what is called "Extrinsic Motivation" for success - that is external motivational factors - Commission, Bonus, Team Competition to win a Holiday etc. These are all examples of extrinsic motivation in action.

However, genuine sustained motivation comes from **within** a person not driven from the outside. That's why adverts for salespeople talk about self-starters and success driven individuals being required.

When the drive to succeed comes from within - known as "Intrinsic Motivation" – it's much more sustainable. It taps into a deeper part of an individual's psyche.

Let me give you an example, again from the sports arena.

What keeps Tiger Woods and Rory McIlroy going? They've got more money than they can use, so it's not that! What keeps Phil "The Power" Taylor going in darts after becoming the World Champion for the 16th time?

Somebody offering money or a trophy to win (extrinsic) is not what drives them on - not really. Yes the cash is nice, the silverware attractive. But their motivation is deeper than that.

In business, what makes an individual like Richard Branson keep going, opening new business ventures as diverse as banking, media and airlines?

Yes I hear you say "ego" and that's part of it but what makes the ego drive a person forward? What makes winning, being the best, being number one - more of a driver, a motivator, than the external rewards that come from being successful?

The answer is found in an individual's wiring. It's all about that personal desire to win. To achieve! In essence to become self-determined and that's what takes over once the lower forms of motivation are taken care of - money, trophies and the accompanying success. If this drive to be self-determined doesn't arise - boredom sets in and careers get cut short.

How many talented young footballers have you witnessed in your favourite football team - who storm into the first eleven - become that season's wonder and then never progress any further? Perhaps due to the "flash" success they get a transfer to a "bigger" club only never to be heard of again? Why does this happen?

The talent doesn't dissipate but the drive, the determination to be the best, does.

They're happy with the money, the lifestyle (show me an 18 year old on 7 grand a week who wouldn't be) and that's where it stops - they've made it - in their own mind. No more drive, no more push to be all they can be. They've reached the "top" of their personal ambition pushed along by extrinsic motivation and then they discover (and so do their coaches and managers) that there's nothing "internal" - no intrinsic drive to make them truly great.

To come back to sales: genuinely, how motivated would you really be by commission if you hit your sales targets all the time - I'm not saying you wouldn't enjoy the money - I'm asking how "motivated" you would be by the targets if they were a doddle, a cinch?

How motivated would Christian Ronaldo be to play, if he lined up against Ryman League division 2 teams for a season (no disrespect to players in that league) - even if he was on the same wage as he was at Real Madrid?

You get the point - extrinsic motivators - money, commission, trophies are all important but they wain as motivators when they are too readily achieved - *if* that's all that's important to the individual.

When the external motivators are achieved the truly motivated individual focusses on the internal reasons for keeping going - that's why sportsmen like Phil Taylor and Tiger Woods keep on winning.

That's how Tiger bounced back from his personal tribulations a few years ago. It wasn't the money - he has more than enough and could've retired to a quiet island somewhere out of the media spotlight. Instead he faced up to the attention that came his way on his return to playing golf (Who's he going out with now? Wonder if he'll stick with his caddy? How's his swing holding up? Will he really be able to get back to the level he was once at?)

Don't you think all that crossed his mind? But what was the result? While the press intrusion would no doubt be a pain, a roadblock in his way, Tiger's desire to get back to being the best golfer in the world drove him on. To him it's now all about accomplishment and success, world records and being the best ever! The extrinsic motivators are secondary.

But guess what?

For the true greats - they always have been secondary!

From day 1 true champions are motivated intrinsically - yes thank you very much for the winnings, the cash, the trophy, the title but let's move on, next please - I've got an itch to scratch, a goal to reach and that is being the best I can be, the best at what I do.

In your sales career - where do you stand?

Are you only extrinsically motivated by your commission or can we get that intrinsic motivation, that self-motivation going? Because let me tell you, when you do - the commission and targets will take care of themselves, they will be a by-product of your internal drive for success and recognition.

So how do we become self-motivated?

Well, it's a combination of three things: Commitment, Goals and a Positive Self Image and all three are interdependent.

So let's start with Commitment.

Commitment

If you're going to become the best in what you do you need to be committed to the process. And it *is* a process, a journey - and depending how far away you are from your destination or your goal - will dictate things such as activities required to reach your goal and the timescales involved.

If you're currently an 18 handicapper at golf and want to play off scratch (0 handicap) you will take longer and need to focus on more things than someone who is playing off a 4 handicap and wants to become scratch. Does that make sense?

So where are you in relation to where you want to be with your sales career?

Just starting out? Been doing it for a while or perhaps years? What do you want from your career? Become the best, most successful in the team? Perhaps your aim is to progress to become Sales Manager or Sales Director?

The first part towards self-motivation is becoming committed to the process and a good way of doing this is to create a **Personal Progress Log**. This will allow you to focus on the tangible areas that require ongoing improvement.

Once again let's look at the sports arena for an example of the above in action:

The Olympic qualifying distance for a male long jumper is 8.20mts. If an athlete is coming up short of this target - let's say 7.90mts - he doesn't just keep practicing by running and jumping over and over hoping to get longer. He practices in the right way. He and/or his coach analyses every area of his performance and works on them in order to improve his performance bit by bit.

For example, the coach will analyse:

Technique: The athlete's Take-off and Landing: is his method correct? Do his hands inadvertently flap around during the jump causing a little drag and resistance, resulting in a loss of distance?

Physical: Does he have enough power in his legs for an explosive run up? If not - into the gym! Leg presses. Resistance training. All designed to put power into those thighs.

Diet: Is he eating properly, is he carrying too many pounds?

Mental: Does he have the belief in himself and his ability or is this holding him back? Does he see himself as an Olympian?

Technical: Is he using the whole run-up area? Is he jumping too soon before the board, causing him to waste vital centimetres in the jump?

You get the point? They don't just keep doing the same thing over and over hoping it will get better.

To keep motivated, you need a *plan of action* and just like our athlete you need to keep track of what you're doing, what your good at and what needs attention - and then work on and practice those areas to improve upon them. The Personal Progress Log helps you do this.

An athlete uses the log to keep track of the areas he's working on and records each activity and progress made. This helps him stay focussed on the key areas requiring improvement and also helps with motivation as he can see how far he's moving along - even if the ultimate goal of 8.20mts has not yet been achieved.

Take gym work for an example; the athlete won't just turn up and start doing leg presses to get stronger thigh muscles, there will be a plan to it:

What are his leg measurements just now? What is the desired target? What can he squat just now (in kilogrammes)? What is the desired amount to increase the muscle mass? By when is this to be achieved?

Now break down all of the areas mentioned previously, Technique, Physical, Diet, Mental, Technical etc. into individual goals and processes and you get a plan of action to move the athlete forward to his ultimate goal of jumping 8.20mts.

This concept has worked for years in the sports arena however; business shouldn't waste time re-inventing the wheel - adopt it and adapt it.

Now, you're not interested in the same areas as the Long Jumper (at least as far as selling skills are concerned) so you need to break your sales role into all of the different components you do day to day, month on month.

On a sheet of paper or spreadsheet write down all the different Disciplines of the Sales role you perform. Items such as; Territory Management & Planning, Making Appointments, Presenting to Customers, Closing the Sale, Market Awareness, Product Knowledge and so on - don't just use these headings - take your time and think about it, include your own sections.

Then once you have all the key sales areas written down, break them into the different facets that make up each discipline.

For example, let's take Presenting to Customers: Under this heading you could have - Building Rapport; Clear understanding of Call Objectives; Knowledge of product features and benefits; Common Objections and Answers; Quality Questions to ask, and so on.

You do this for all areas of the sales role you perform. Just like the long jumper, you're focussing on the key areas that will make you a successful salesperson.

Once done, rate yourself honestly for each of the different disciplines and facets you have created.

Rate each area A, B or C.

A: perfect, no need to act upon it.

B: acceptable performance level but could improve - all the way down to . . .

C: Poor at this discipline!

Also, take a leaf from the athlete's personal progress log - when applicable make targets specific, list them numerically. For example:

A= 6 calls per day, B=4 calls per day, C = less than 4

A=4 new prospects per week, B=3 new prospects, C=2 or less

This avoids doubt and makes the goal tangible.

So what's the point of the progress log?

Commitment to improvement!

You commit yourself to removing the "C's" one by one (don't take on too many at one time, else they'll not improve). Then once they're all removed, turn your attention to moving the "B's" up to "A's".

Remember my comment earlier about people in driving ranges practicing what they are good at? It may make you feel good but it won't improve your performance as much as working on your weaknesses. A self-development tool such as a Personal Progress Log will help you record and set goals to improve your all round sales game.

If you do this correctly, you will have a blueprint that will last you for years and help you improve each and every aspect of your sales abilities. Each one will be a goal - a personal target to be monitored and improved upon and will get you on your way to the success you desire.

Goals

As mentioned earlier, a long jumper doesn't just keep running and jumping over and over again in order to achieve 8.20mts. If they're coming up short they and their coach will analyse each and every aspect of the long jumper's performance to find areas of improvement and then set achievable goals in each department to encourage improvement and gain confidence through continued success as each goal is achieved.

They're not looking to improve from 7.90 metres to 8.20 meters in one go! Every centimetre gained is a success and builds the athlete's confidence.

Do you see a similarity?

Sales people are Corporate Athletes. You need to keep fit for the competition; else you'll be left behind. Even if you know the most about your industry or product - there's more than one factor to being an athlete – and there's more than one element to being a Sales Person.

By getting committed and using a Personal Progress Log, you'll be focussing on goals and improvements that will see you improve bit by bit, until others are chasing you.

But your goals do not need to be limited to skill improvements tied to your sales role.

What do you want out of life? This year? Next year?

What about health goals, fitness goals, education goals? Monetary goals? Career goals?

They are all valid vehicles for moving an individual forward in life and should be used to help you.

But remember this - Goals you set need to be desired by you! Not your partner, your parents, your children nor any significant other. They have to be yours.

But why?

Because you have to believe in them, want them, desire them. They need to be yours so you will dream about them, focus on them and think about them each and every day.

They are your intrinsic motivators, the reason you do what you do.

There are books galore on goal setting if you don't know how to go about establishing them, so I won't labour the point here as the purpose of me mentioning setting goals is to relate them to the inner motivation winners have, as without goals or having a purpose you'll find it hard to stay motivated when the going gets tough.

What do you think keeps the long jumper jumping? The training? The long days in the gym? Perhaps. But it's more likely his vision; the goal of him standing on the podium hearing the national anthem being played while looking down proudly at the gold medal around his neck.

That's what keeps him going when he feels low, tired or just not up for training that day.

This is the same inner drive that made Paul Lawrie stand in freezing weather, having cleared snow away from the driving range north of Aberdeen, where he was the professional and hit ball after ball, day in and day out in the wind, rain and snow; dreaming, believing that one day he would win a major golf tournament.

And guess what? The conditions came to meet him one July evening in 1999, when he managed to battle the wind and rain that seen off many a so called better player during the last round of the Open at Carnoustie.

That Sunday was Lawrie's weather - *his* time had arrived - just like he dreamt it would during those long winter hours on the range.

Goals keep you focussed. They tell you what you want out of life and as I mentioned earlier you should set goals across all areas of your life:

Work, Financial, Relationships, Health, Personal, Recreational

It's down to you. But be warned - just thinking about something nice for a moment does not make it a goal.

Goal Setting Technique

1. You must want it, desire it. It doesn't matter if right now you don't know how you'll get it. You just need to want it with a passion because if you don't it will simply be a delightful wish - not a goal.

2. You must make the goal tangible - what is called SMART; Specific, Measureable, Attractive, Relevant and Time Bound. Put another way; what do you want? Make it as clear and specific as possible (size, colour, how much etc. etc.), why do you want it and by when?

3. Write goals down. Read them every day. Visualise them. Dream about them. Want them. Allow the RAS to help you find ways to attain them. It will.

4. Break your goals into smaller chunks and steps and make them your yearly, monthly and daily plan or to-do list. You should ask yourself EVERY DAY - is what I'm doing getting me closer to my goal and if it's not, stop doing it and get focussed.

5. Make at least one goal a **real stretcher**. Perhaps one that will take you right out of your comfort zone and truly work out how and by when you will achieve it.

6. Make at least one of your goals a "breakthrough goal" a "keystone goal", a goal that really means something to you, one that will give you such a

boost when it's achieved, it will propel you onto greater things. Once set, make sure you do at least 2 or 3 things - 2 or 3 activities big or small, to move you forward towards that goal every day until you achieve it.

By its very nature your breakthrough or keystone goal should be challenging, tough and inspiring. You want to push yourself and prove to yourself this goal setting game works.

A big win gives you that confidence.

I can't tell you what goals to set or why, all I can do is advise you of why you should do it.

Think of your mind as a Satnav. You know where you are now and your goals are programming your desired destination. Every action you take from now on will lead you towards your destination or away from it. If you truly desire your goal - just like top sportspeople do - the thought of it will drive you on when the going gets tough, it'll keep you focussed and remind you of why you are doing what you do.

Also, don't forget many goals follow on from each other and are reliant upon one another. If you want the bigger house and car and executive salary, then your career goals - when attained - will provide the lifestyle you want. The goals you set for your career, will aid the financial goals and so on.

I appreciate that some of you may have tried setting goals before and they may not have worked and so are a bit sceptical of the whole thing.

Well, while I appreciate your point of view, please remember that less than 10% of people set themselves real goals and only 3% of those write them down and break them down into specific tasks and actions. So the majority of those people you meet, socialise with or are related to - don't set goals. That's the norm, the average. They're in league with the millions of people throughout the world who are permanently on the periphery of greatness, all at the beck and call and mercy of those who *do* have a plan.

Those who have no goals of their own normally work for those who do and help *them* achieve *their* goals without even knowing it.

So make your selling matter each and every day. There are not many areas in industry and commerce where someone can stand out as a "star". Selling, fortunately, allows for talent to shine as every company out there wants someone who can create business and make money, so you've chosen a great career to define and attain personal goals and when you start to achieve them you'll feel good about it - really good - because it didn't happen by accident, you planned it.

And how you feel is directly linked to the third aspect of self-motivation I mentioned earlier, which is having a Positive Self Image.

Positive Self Image

Nothing beats feeling good about yourself and while you can attempt to hide your true feelings from others - you can't hide them from yourself!

This links directly to the self-talk we looked at in Chapter 1. So it's imperative we constantly "top up" our self-image, our self-esteem and nothing does this better, than being successful.

Think about it, if you're improving and developing you'll naturally, intrinsically, feel good because you're growing as a person and improving all the while.

Then, just as you sense these intrinsic feelings of success - you'll also be winning, reaching targets and making money because of your goals and commitments and consequently you'll be achieving extrinsic goals as well.

All of which forms a neat little circle of success that makes you feel good about yourself - not necessarily because of the cash (although nice to have) but because you've accomplished what you set out to achieve and you've reinforced your internal Positive Self-Image - and others will see and feel that when in your presence.

Just look at every world class sportsperson and you will see an air of self-belief and confidence - yes some do carry that over into arrogance and I'm not advocating that but that's more down to their individual personality than the fact they are full of self-belief.

In sales, self-belief brings confidence, not only to the individual sales person but to those who will deal with you; your colleagues, your customers and your prospects.

So to get your journey in having a Positive Self Image started I'd like to suggest a little exercise.

Take some time out and get a piece of paper and a pen (or your laptop or iPad) and divide your life into 3 stages.

If you're 30 years old do Birth to 10, 11 to 20 and 21 to 30. If you're 54, do birth to 18, 19 to 36 and 37 to 54 and so on. Simply divide your age into three "chapters" of your life to date.

Now write down 3 things; 3 successes you've had in each age group. These can be personal, career, health, family orientated - it doesn't matter. Obviously your achievements at school may not be as "big" as later in life but what stood out at that age? Don't dismiss the small "wins".

Once you've done 3, could you revisit the list and do 5 in each group or more? Don't fret over it if you can't, just focus on what you've achieved to date and write down what you can.

So how many have you got? How many successes?

Be honest, some you had forgotten about, hadn't you? Some you probably didn't "rate" until you thought about it. Yet all were successes. In other words, without even being aware of it, you've proven you can be successful.

So what do you think you could achieve with the planning, organisation and determination that setting goals brings?

Keep that list handy. Read it often. As you progress towards your goals, don't neglect to mark off your new successes each and every day.

End each day by reflecting on what's happened, what you completed, what's moved you a step closer to your goal and take credit for it. You planned it and did it - no one else.

Taking note of your successes, even little ones, is vital because every day you'll hit roadblocks - problems and issues that will attempt to derail you - but don't let them.

Stay focussed on your goals.

Some days you'll sail along, others you'll feel like you're coming to a shuddering halt but stay focussed on your prize and you'll reach your destination.

Sylvester Stallone was rejected and rejected and rejected when he was trying to sell his screenplay "Rocky". The issue wasn't with the script; it was Stallone's insistence on playing the lead role himself. That was his goal. His dream. An unknown actor, who sounded like he had a speech impediment wanted to play the lead in a movie he had written!

As the months progressed he continued to receive offers to buy the script but he turned them down one after another. Eventually he found a producer and a company who was willing to take a punt but at a price - a meagre budget of just over $1million - in Hollywood terms this was a definite "B" movie in the making. But Sylvester Stallone didn't care, he had his dream.

Rocky took just 28 days to film and went on to earn over $ 225 million dollars. It won Oscars for best picture, best director and best editing as well as acting and screenplay nominations for Stallone and as they say, the rest is history.

Between the Rocky and Rambo series of films, Stallone has grossed over $2Billion at the Box Office and has went on to have a long and successful career.

Do you think he envisaged his movies making Billions of dollars?

Perhaps. But it's more likely he was focussed on one thing, playing Rocky Balboa in the movie he had written. That was his dream, his focus. And when it happened - the fame, success and money followed.

What a great example of self-belief and determination to achieve a goal.

And it's an example seen and repeated throughout time across many differing areas of industry, commerce and sport. Every sector has examples of people who defied the odds and won because of their determination to reach their goal.

Back in April 2011 Rory McIlroy stood on the 10th Tee during the final round of the Masters leading the field by 4 shots. The 22 year old had led the tournament for three consecutive rounds and now stood only 9 holes away from his first major victory.

This is what he had dreamt about all his days and his dream was on the verge of becoming a reality.

Then disaster struck. A severe hook (pull to the left) off the 10th tee sent his ball out of bounds and bit by bit his game unravelled, dropping him from first place to eventually finishing tied 15th.

Afterwards, the pundits had a field day analysing the young Irishman. Would he ever come back from such a disaster? Was this the end of his career before it had really begun? How would he turn this around? Could he?

The world - and the pundits - didn't have long to wait for an answer.

On the 19th of June - only nine weeks after his Masters debacle - Rory McIlroy won his first major championship, the US Open, by 8 clear strokes.

No mean feat to win by such a margin when up against a world class field. But that was only part of the story. He didn't just beat the golfing elite he was up against - he re-wrote the record books:

- Lowest ever score in a US Open -16 under par

- Fastest player to 11 under – 27 holes

- Lowest 36 hole score at a US Open – 11 under par

- Lowest 54 hole Score at a US Open – 14 under par

- 62 out of 72 Greens in Regulation – a US record

Not bad for a 22 year old who had seen his game desert him, leaving him dejected and humiliated only a few weeks before.

McIlroy's 2011 US Open victory was all about head, heart and guts. He hadn't become a bad golfer overnight. He knew that and his team knew that. He dug deep and reconnected with himself, firing up his self-belief - his intrinsic motivation seeing him through the trauma and onto victory.

And we can all learn from the young Ulsterman's experience.

Remember, self-motivation comes from within. Don't rely solely on external triggers. Become committed to your own self-improvement and setting your own goals. Believe in yourself. Believe in your dream.

Although I've briefly alluded to it, here's not the place to go into detail about how to set SMART goals and objectives - you can look that up easily on the web - this chapter is about re-establishing the value of setting them and what focus it can bring you.

Your values in life tell you why you want to do a thing. Goals and Objectives tell you what and when. And your daily tasks tell you how.

Take time. Get connected to yourself.

There's not one world class performer who's not taken the time to set out and plan the road they travel. It's their guidance system for when they get lost.

Reflections on Mental Skill Number 2:

Analyse the sales role you perform. Break it down into its components and create a Personal Progress Log for yourself.

Then take some time and set yourself goals and objectives for improvement at work, personal life and any other area you wish to have success in.

Identify a breakthrough or keystone goal and work towards it.

Make a plan to achieve your goals and reflect on your successes daily, no matter how small.

Mental Skill Number 3:

Managing Anxiety, Stress and Emotions

Mental Skill Number 3: Managing Anxiety, Stress and Emotions

This is one of the most important mental skills professional sportspeople employ and it can definitely help you in your role as a sales professional.

Discussing Anxiety and Stress may seem negative but the fact is we can all get anxious and stressed when faced with situations out with what we consider our "norm".

When selling, especially if the sale isn't going according to plan or is much bigger than you're normally used to, you can be under pressure and that can impact on your performance.

So in this chapter we will look at how you can utilise mental techniques to help you cope with difficult situations you may encounter when selling.

It could be argued that anyone with the required level of skill can perform any given task:

A professional golfer can hole 3 foot putt after 3 foot putt on the practice green.

A professional footballer can score penalty after penalty on the training ground.

A salesperson can write up order after order on their regular daily route.

But inherent, natural skills can easily come under immense pressure and go to pot when faced with different circumstances.

Take the same 3 foot putt but this time for the Open, the Claret Jug and £1m pounds.

The penalty; same distance from goal, same weight of ball but this time to win the World Cup in front of 60,000 baying fans!

And what about the sale that's 10, 20, 50 times larger than normal? Or the prospect, who's making you jump through hoops and hitting you with every objection under the sun?

Now, given these circumstances, the easy well practiced skills are under immense pressure and it's not uncommon for them to fail. How many times have you heard the unkind expression; "he bottled it!"

Skills and mental agility suffer when **emotions** come into play, especially when anxiety and stress are present but even too much excitement can lead to a failure in performance as the mind interferes with the ability to think straight and perform even basic motor skills. I have seen it happen to Sportsmen and Women across many sports and also to Salespeople - who have been shaking like a leaf at the thought of giving a presentation to a group of prospects.

But let's clear one thing up before we go any further - everyone gets nervous. It's all a matter of why and when *and* how to control it.

When it comes to Sports and Selling, the most common manifestation of stress can be attributed to what is called **Performance Anxiety**.

For example, one golfer may experience anxiety about getting off the first tee in the monthly medal in front of his friends. Another may be anxious about making the cut, to another it's about keeping his winning streak going.

Three totally different "concerns" but each one manifesting itself through anxiety and worry to some degree.

Some salespeople get anxious about talking on the phone, they much prefer face to face. Others get extremely nervous when it comes to Closing the Sale, especially if the process has taken a long while and they've invested a lot of time and effort in it. They're afraid it'll all come to nothing if they don't get the order.

Other salespeople dread the Price Objection and live in fear of it being raised by the prospect and you can see them physically deflate when the price is mentioned.

So what's going on mentally and how do you combat it?

All of the examples given above result in stress and more specifically, anxiety.

Anxiety is an unpleasant emotion, which is normally accompanied by a vague but persistent feeling of apprehension and dread - it can create a state of worry, tension and even fear.

There are two main types of "anxiety" to be considered when looking at Performance:

First is Trait Anxiety:

Individuals who have Trait Anxiety characteristics are normally viewed as being "anxiety prone" throughout life in general and it should come as no surprise to someone who has a Trait Anxiety personality that they will experience anxiety on a regular bases. That's the downside.

The upside is, to you - anxiety is a "normal" state.

You live with it every day, so it's perfectly reasonable to accept that "one more anxiety trigger" will not have the same negative impact on you as it would on someone who is not wired this way.

So, when it comes to Performance in sport and in sales, we are normally dealing with the other type of anxiety which is:

State Anxiety:

This is a temporary, situation-specific form of apprehension.

Now it actually doesn't matter whether you are anxious about making a fool of yourself on the first tee, keeping your winning streak going or are anxious about talking on the phone or closing the sale - you are experiencing typical State Anxiety. Allow the feelings of dread to take over and you may end up getting what you're worrying about (you'll top the ball off the tee, or lose the sale).

As mentioned before, the term "choking" is often used when feelings of anxiety take over.

So why does it happen?

Quite simply, you face a decrease in performance. The ability to think and perform what should be routine tasks and skills diminishes - due to too much perceived stress regarding the situation you find yourself in. And the key word here is "**perceived**". The Stress is all in your mind. It's the result of how *you're* interpreting the situation.

You see it's not normally the "external situation" that causes the stress but the way we think about it - that's what creates feelings of anxiety and fear.

There are exceptions of course - being hunted by a wild animal or a mad man with a gun - yes it's the situation in this instance that's causing the fear - but honestly, how many salespeople have been killed for asking for the order?

This can be explained by a simple formula that I read a few years ago: E+R=O - Event + Response = Outcome.[2]

Let's say I tell you you're the worst salesperson I've ever met. (That's the event).

Now you have a choice.

Perhaps your self-talk is saying "God he's good. He's only known me 5 minutes and he's sussed me out already" or you could be saying, "What? Nice one pal. I think you've got me mixed up with someone else; quite an error for someone supposedly into Psychology!"

Two different responses to the same event and depending which one you say to yourself internally will dictate the outcome - how you feel afterwards.

You see it's not what I say to you that really matters - it's what *you* say to you that counts.

You cannot control the external world around you, the people in it or the things that they do - the only thing you are directly in control of is you, your thoughts and your reactions and responses.

Does that make sense?

When you truly accept this principle you are taking responsibility for everything you feel and do because you understand it's ultimately down to you to determine how you feel and react in any given situation.

In other words you take full responsibility for your life and leave behind the days of being up and down and pulled around mentally due to other people's actions.

What they do does not concern you.

What they think of you does not concern you.

What they say does not concern you.

What does concern you is what *you* do - how *you* react - when they do or say something to you. The power to dictate the outcome is in *your* hands.

When they're angry towards you - remember it's really the situation or late delivery that they are angry about, they just happen to be venting at you.

When they question the price, they may well be happy with it and are just seeking clarification that will help them to justify the spend to their superiors.

Do not automatically see the negative in every given situation. Try to respond positively and see how that makes you and them feel.

For salespeople who experience Performance Anxiety it's important to remember that you can control the thoughts you have regarding the situation you are in. You can change your response and so get a better outcome.

But remember we are all different - what suits one person will not suit another when it comes to modifying our reactions, so it's important to create a "package" of actions, activities and routines that will suit you and your personality.

Here are some ideas that you may wish to adopt - they will help you cope when faced with situations that cause you stress and anxiety. But do not limit yourself just to these. Think of your own as well.

Ways of dealing with Performance Anxiety before the Sales Call:

Should you find yourself getting uptight about the sales call (the event) try some of the following techniques (your response) to help you relax and get over your anxiety?

Remember - it's all in your mind!

Arrive at the prospect with plenty of time so you're not rushed. Running around two minutes before your appointment like a blue assed fly will only increases your stress levels.

Make sure you have everything you need; brochures, samples, paperwork, figures etc.

Take time to check your plan for the call. What are your objectives for this meeting?

Go over the questions you will ask, make sure the brochures are in their allocated place in your bag - this can be built in to routine that sends signals to your brain that will get it into the correct relaxed positive mode for selling.

As you go into the Customer or Prospect:

If you're feeling nervous for any reason, understand that your nerves are normal and accept them, especially during important calls.

Don't fight the adrenalin or nervous energy you feel, this is not fear, it's anticipation. Acknowledge it but don't focus on it. Once you begin selling, the feeling will subside as you get into the process.

As you sit in reception, allow yourself a few minutes to visualize yourself doing everything right. Think back to a call where everything went according to plan. Enjoy the feeling of success. Let it sink in and enhance your self-image and self-esteem.

Breathe deeply and easily.

Have an air of confidence. You've practiced. You know your stuff.

When with the Customer:

Should Performance Anxiety raise its head during the call, perhaps due to a couple of awkward questions or even a demo failure, try the following strategies to help you regain composure and confidence, remember it's your **response** that will ultimately dictate the outcome:

Focus on the process of the sale rather than the outcome. We'll discuss this in detail later on but it's about letting go of what the sale means (the outcome) just focus on what's next in the process or what you need to do to get back on track.

Stay present and "in the moment" and avoid thinking too far into the sale or thinking about your commission at the end.

The most important thing at present that needs your full attention is the statement you're about to make or question you're about to ask, not your success at the end. That will take care of itself should you take care of the process of selling.

If you find yourself thinking negative thoughts or engage in negative self-talk, stop and focus only on your breathing and engage your peripheral vision - *I'll describe this in a moment*. This will automatically pull you back into the present, regain focus and begin working on the process.

If you say something the prospect disagrees with or finds fault in, remember one bad shot doesn't make a bad round! Don't get down. Don't send reinforcement signals to the brain that will make it remember the mistake. Ask the customer what he or she would prefer - if what you say is not acceptable. Buy time. Put the ball back in their court.

Ways of dealing with Anxiety after the call:

If you feel anxious or down after the sales call or even if you feel elated, review the following suggestions to either dismiss the negative feelings (remove their power) or reinforce and strengthen what went right, so it will become easier to draw upon it in the future.

In the car, review the sales call and recall the things you did well. If it helps write them down in a diary or IPad/laptop etc.

Focus on the actions, thoughts and behaviours that helped you. This is a form of mental rehearsal where you practice skills that will be used during your next call.

Acknowledge, but quickly dismiss things that went wrong. Focusing on negative aspects of the meeting will not help you improve in time for the next immanent call. But you *must* have the ability to improve and not make the same mistake over and over.

If you are anxious because of persistent mistakes and keep slipping up with the same error, perhaps it should become part of your Personal Progress Log as discussed previously? Review this at home not in the car and make appropriate arrangements and set goals to improve this area of performance.

In Summary; in order to manage Performance Anxiety it's important that you identify what you're anxious about.

Know your own triggers and remember that stress is all in the mind! You cannot dictate fully what will happen in a call, during a presentation or when you are with a prospect but you can plan and prepare as best you can and be fully aware of your responses.

If you do get nervous, try to interpret the pre-call anxious signals constructively. View the feelings as almost a prerequisite to a good performance. How do you think Footballers feel before the Champions League Final? Exactly! Everyone gets nervous at some time or other.

Nerves show that the match or in your case, the sales call, matters to you - focus and view the feelings as positive rather than negative. You're human, congratulations!

When possible, use relaxation techniques to relieve tension and keep the rhythm that you require to perform well and use "positive self-talk" to help you focus on the process and remain in the present.

So to finish off this section, here's a secret technique athletes use to stay calm and get focussed.

You're probably aware that taking long, slow, deep breaths helps you to reduce tension. However, there is a downside to using this technique - people around you see you doing it (and so know you're uptight) and it takes time for controlled breathing to reduce your heart rate and invoke relaxation - it's not quick! So standing or sitting in a reception area, panting and puffing away to yourself while you wait for the prospect to appear is not a recommended way of imparting confidence in those that may see you!

But thankfully there is another way to control any nerves or tension you may be experiencing.

Consider sprinters, staring up the track as they wait for the 100mts final to commence or High Jumpers staring at the bar as they rock back and forth on their heels before commencing their run up. Next time you see this happening - look closely at their eyes. They almost look "spaced out".

What they're doing is engaging their peripheral vision to become relaxed, calm and centred as they visualise performing their task. It's a technique that's fast, effective and almost imperceptible to others around, unless they look very closely - and by engaging their peripheral vision, the athletes gain instant calmness, focus and composure.

Read the following few paragraphs and then try the technique.

Find a point straight in front of you and focus on it. Now gradually become aware of what's around it . . . . Let your vision spread out in front of you to the corners of the room while keeping your gaze on the chosen point. As you do this, you'll become more and more aware of the periphery of your vision. Just let it happen.

Let your senses of hearing, touch, smell and spatial awareness spread out to the periphery as well. Notice any physiological changes that are happening to you as you do it. Just let them happen. Relax into it.

Your jaw may become heavier, your breathing deeper in your chest, your shoulders, heavy and relaxed.

Just keep staring at the chosen point and let your vision widen. . . . Keep feeling relaxed and focussed.

Now, when you're ready, bring your attention back to the point you were looking at and you will quickly get back into normal focus but feel calm, centred and ready for action.

Why not try this a few times until you get the hang of it?

Being relaxed is one of the most important fundamentals of performing well and it's hard to be relaxed and calm when your heart is pumping, your breathing is rapid and you're uptight and frustrated with all around you.

Using your peripheral vision is one quick way of getting your heart rate down and so be in the right frame of mind to perform.

Professional athletes use it all the time to benefit their performance. So should you.

Reflections on Mental Skill Number 3:

Consider some of the techniques to control nerves and anxiety before, during and after a sales call.

What will you practice and develop?

List your action points below:

Mental Skill Number 4:

Working your Game Plan & Concentration

Mental Skill Number 4:

Working on your Game Plan & Maintaining Concentration

When it comes to sport you're probably aware of sayings such as "having a game plan" in football or "excellent course management" in golf; but what do they mean?

Essentially it's about having a strategy that will see the player or team successfully negotiate the match or game and overcome their opponents.

It's not about altering a player's skill - that doesn't change - it's about how they approach the up and coming event, ensuring they give themselves the best opportunity to win.

For example, when football teams come up against FC Barcelona in the European Champions League, it's not uncommon for them to let the Catalan's have most of the play while they set up defensively to avoid a heavy defeat - whereas on the Saturday they might be the stronger team and be more attack minded in their own league.

Now you may view the above example as a team displaying "negative" tactics; they're afraid of Barca so they "shut up shop" and put eleven men behind the ball. And I couldn't argue with that point of view, it is a negative tactic - but the big picture has to be looked at by the opposition coach.

In the Champions' League Group stages it's a "round robin" set up - the four teams play each other twice, so avoiding a heavy defeat is imperative as qualifying out of the group may come down to goal difference if the points are equal. That's why a 1-0 defeat is better than 4-1. The team still loses the 3 points but they are better off goal wise.

Now the same team playing Barca in the knockout stages, may well adopt a more cavalier approach to the game, especially when playing at home. In this instance, they know the game is decided over two legs against the same team - not over six games in a mini league.

Same two teams involved but one employing an alternative game plan because of different circumstance.

It's the same with golfers. How players approach the Master's each year is totally different to playing the British Open. The courses are totally different and need to be managed in different ways - there are places you just don't want to put the golf ball because it will cost you shots and therefor your chance of winning.

The Golfers still use the same skills to strike the ball, play bunker shots and so on but whereas they may send the ball high in Augusta at the Masters, they may hit it lower to stay under the wind on a links course in the UK. They need the skills to be able do that but a game plan, a strategy to carry it out successfully.

So when it comes to selling – what's your game plan?

Is it simply to chap on as many doors or phone as many numbers as possible and see what happens? *Can be valid in certain circumstances!* Or are you more of a strategist, using the Internet, LinkedIn, Trade Directories, Networking Groups and so on?

I've no doubt the approach will depend on your industry. All I'm asking of you is to think about how you're currently doing it. Is it working? Can it be improved upon? Should it be the same for every prospect or do you need to adapt and be more flexible?

There's a powerful saying I heard a few years back and I believe that it's so true.

Do what you've been doing and you'll get what you've got!

You're where you are today because of the decisions you have made and the actions you've taken in the past. If you're happy with how it's going - then well done - keep doing it.

If not - if it could be better - if you feel you could have much more success, then you need to change something because as I mentioned, if you keep doing what you're doing, you'll keep getting what you've got.

In previous chapters we have looked at Self-Image and Confidence and how to foster them. Well now's the time to put them into action.

Question Why? Why? Why?

Why are you doing things the way you are if results are not improving?

Why do you work your territory the way you do?

Why do you only rely only on cold calling to find prospects?

Why do long term sales cycles get you frustrated?

I could go on and on giving examples but the key is that you must constantly ask why?

Challenge yourself.

Get out of your comfort zone. Remember 90% of what you do day to day is HABIT. The more you challenge your automatic processes, the more in control and confident you'll become.

So if the above makes sense, why do so many people just keep doing what they've always done, even though it's not successful and may even be harming their prospects in life - keeping them in debt or constantly seeing promotion passing them by?

Yes, it could simply be down to habits that are hard to shake but it's more likely to be a lack of belief in themselves first and foremost, coupled with a lack of conviction that the change they are thinking of making will be beneficial to them. God forbid, the change might even bring "pain". The new approach may not work. The prospect may not be there at the event and I'll waste my time. The market doesn't sell that way.

Excuses, excuses, excuses - all caused by a lack of real Self-Belief.

Sure the approach may not be right for your market but unless you try it - how do you know?

And if it doesn't work, simply move on. Find another way and another way and another way. One will pay dividends, that's for sure. It just a question of your will power to keep on trying and looking for ways to constantly improve.

When a method doesn't work - it does not mean failure. It simply means that way is not suitable. So find another!

Too simple?

Then why not try it. Sit down and think of as many ways you could do things differently in your current sales role. Plan and prepare. Write them down and commit to trying those that make sense (some of your ideas may well be crazy but don't let that stop you). Research your ideas, prioritize them. Put them into action.

Antony Robins, the author of programmes such as Get the Edge and Personal Power has a great saying:

"Success leaves clues"

Think about it; almost everything you may want to do in life has already been done by someone else.

Someone has already thought about it, planned it and done it and in their wake left clues that can be found on the Internet, in books, manuals and audio and video programs, training events, seminars, and workshops.

Think differently and go and see if your ideas will work. There are clues out there.

Sportsmen and women throughout the world constantly look for new ways to improve, to get the edge over their competitors; Diets, Training Regimes, Mental Strength Training and using technology in innovative ways, for example. They're willing to do anything; they'll go the extra mile to win.

And all the while, they're simply seeking an advantage that will put them $1/10,000^{th}$ of a second in front or one stroke ahead.

Remember, in sport winning can come down to the smallest of margins but when you bring that same attitude to selling *you* will be *way* ahead of the competition, not just a fraction - because you will be one of the early pioneers that's adopting and adapting powerful mental techniques in the sales industry. You will be different. You will stand out.

I'm not sure if it was Einstein who said the definition of insanity is to keep doing the same thing over and over and expect different results!

It doesn't happen that way!

If you're happy with your achievements to date, if you're where you want to be in life - then congratulations - well done, enjoy the remainder of this book and simply keep doing what you've been doing and you'll keep replicating the same results.

But if you're not - **CHANGE THINGS!**

Get your plan, your strategy together and move onwards towards your goals. Look to incorporate challenging ideas that will move you forward. That's what you need to do from this moment on.

So how do you go about creating a game plan in sales that will give you a strategy for success?

What is right for your individual circumstances depends on your ability, outlook and even the industry you work in.

For example, some sales are completed in a day, 10 minutes even; while others can take years to bring to fruition. So the strategy and game plan required to work through a sale that takes months will obviously be different to one that's repeated daily.

However, we can work through the process of creating a game plan and you can then adapt it to suit your own personal circumstances.

Fully understand your sales process.

Let's start at the beginning.

What do you go through to complete a sale from scratch?

Does it involve Prospecting? If so - how do you do it? How often? Challenge the status quo: are there other ways/better ways to find prospects? Are you aware of them? Have you explored them all?

On the point of prospecting, I'm a great believer that we actually begin the sales process looking at "suspects" not prospects! You *suspect* they might buy from you but only once you know they are in the market or are open to discussion about your offerings do they become genuine prospects. If they're not going to buy because they've just signed a 5 year deal with one of your competitors - they are only a live prospect when they are looking to renew the contract in 4 ½ years' time.

Now I'm not saying don't keep in contact with them but you can't treat them like a prospect that's in the market *now* for what you're selling!

So you've found your prospect - what's next? You visit them to establish is there a Need? In other words do you do a Fact Find mission?

Once again, think about your approach. Are you successful at getting in the door? Could it work better? What other methods could you utilize to engage prospects? LinkedIn? Networking events? Attending exhibitions?

What do you say to get an appointment? Does it work? Could you do it differently, more efficiently?

Once in with the prospect what questions do you ask? Do you rattle off questions like an Inquisitor, leaving the prospect shell-shocked and reluctant to see you again or do you engage in building rapport, attempting to understand how they're "wired" so you can tailor your approach when presenting your solution?

If your sale traditionally happens during one call and you find many prospects say no - you may play a numbers game - 10 calls, 2 orders etc.

So why not mix things up a little, consider trying a 2 call strategy?

The first call is a fact find; you build rapport and then make an appointment as you leave to return with a proposal. This psychological "shift" takes pressure off you to close on the first call and also makes the prospect more relaxed and perhaps more open to what you're proposing, as you went away and took the time to consider their requirements.

The above may work - it may not. But have you though it through? Tried it with a few prospects to see the results?

If your traditional way of attempting to close the deal in one call gives you an average of 2 orders every 10 calls and going back twice produces a ratio of 6 orders every 20 calls (same 10 customers - only seen twice) the strategy works. You've improved your closing rate by 50%.

Remember, question, question, question everything you've done up until this point. Why is it done that way? Perhaps the answer you'll get is simply, "because that's the way it has always been done".

What about a longer sales cycle? How do you get them turned onto what you are selling? How do you control the passing of time? What reasons do you have to keep on calling on the prospect to ensure the competition is kept at bay?

How long does this part of the sales process take? 5 visits? 6 months? A year?

If this is your type of selling, only you can answer that but however long it takes - it's all about determining your sales process and what you should be planning to do at each stage.

Think of a golfer. Their caddie has walked the course and measured pin placements for each day. The two of them have played a few practice rounds before the tournament begins. The player will have hit shots from numerous angles onto the greens, working out the best place to land the ball for the easiest putt regardless of the pin locations.

Nothing is left to chance. Club selection for the course (long irons or hybrids for low penetrating flight or high soft landings), distances and pin locations, what type of shots to play etc. they are all considered and factored into the game plan. And next week it all begins again but perhaps with different decisions being made.

Different course, different clubs and perhaps even different weather but the same approach to the game plan strategy.

So does your sales cycle vary industry by industry, sector by sector or is it the same timeframe regardless? Does your plan need to factor in variables?

What's next in your sales process? Do you generate a Quote - a Proposal to be taken back in and then Close the Sale?

Does it go to Tender? Does your proposals go to Management Boards or Committees? Have you tried to get in there and do a presentation or is the decision made behind closed doors? How can you influence things?

Once more, asking questions of yourself and your process may give you ideas that will prove more beneficial than the way it's done now.

As part of the sales process, do you get involved in Negotiation or are the prices fixed or based on volume? Are your skills and confidence as high as they should be? What can be done differently to help you win?

Only **you** can define your current sales process but you must do it - it keeps you on track with the sale and what you should be doing next. It's your map of the sale and helps you identify activities that work and those that don't, so you can constantly develop and improve them.

I have one client whose typical sales cycle is 3 years from the start to getting the order. To keep track of this, every member of the sales team has a document entitled "Milestones for Success". In it - it outlines activities that need to be done 36 months from tender, 24 months, 12 months, 6 months right up to the Tender date.

This is their Game Plan for winning Tenders, without it important activities may be missed while more immediate potential orders are chased.

Of course, they also have customers who don't go to Tender, so use a totally different game plan for them.

However, the message is clear. Know your Sales Process or Processes and create your game plan - it's your strategy to help you win more business. Then once you have created and mapped your sales process - once it's in play, monitor it. If it's working, stick to it - if not, tweak it; adjust it so it does work.

Don't be afraid to ask different questions, trying different ways to prospect or demo your products. The more options you have at your disposal, the more chances you have to succeed.

Once again, in Sales we can learn from the Sports arena in this respect. Know your skills and abilities but be ready to adapt your game plan to suit what's in front of you.

Identify your Patterns

So you've got a game plan in place but what about you as an individual?

Are there times of day when you're more alive than others? Are you a morning person or an evening person? Are you happier doing new business development or account management?

We all have our strengths and weaknesses and should try to work *to* our strengths and *on* our weaknesses.

If you're a morning person and have a major deal to close, I'd suggest making the appointment in the morning. It makes sense to play to your strengths, yes? But if that's not possible, if the client will only see you late afternoon - then at least ensure you are up for it. Take whatever steps are necessary to be as alert as you can be during the meeting.

That may seem like common sense but I can't count the number of times I've been out and about with salespeople who leave the most important call to last. Yes they want to finish on a high, I get that. But by the time they get there, having done a day's work prospecting, selling, receiving setbacks and having driven nearly 100 miles - they are shattered! I can sense it, they definitely can feel it and now they are about to make the sales call that will make or break their day or even month!

Planning. Planning. Planning.

To be successful, planning and prioritising must form part of your routine. I know the customer can dictate the appointment time but what you do leading up to it directly affects your performance. Perhaps making this important call on another day would have been more appropriate, a day where you could have chosen an earlier time?

Assertiveness is a skill that successful men and women possess in both sports and in business. They're aware of what works for them and plan accordingly. They are not afraid to use the word "no" in order to ensure they attain what's important for them and their priorities.

Now I'm not suggesting you refuse to go to appointments! Just that you're in charge of your diary, your week, your life.

Make sure you plan around your goals. Treat customers as equals. You are there to help them, save them money, make them more efficient or whatever it is your product or service does for them. They deserve your full and uninhibited attention, so plan to see them when you can offer them the best of you.

How confident would you be being operated on by a surgeon who had just worked 14 hours straight? Or getting into a taxi whose driver looked like he was ready to fall asleep due to the long hours he's pulled? You wouldn't be confident or comfortable at all would you?

So always plan to perform at your best.

Manage your time and territory well.

Perhaps incorporate some goals that will help improve alertness and stamina if you feel yourself flagging towards the end of the day when there's still work to be done. Alternatively, remember to use relaxation techniques such as engaging your peripheral vision. A few minutes in this state will help you become rejuvenated and be up for the task in hand.

When it comes to identifying patterns, do you handle too many things at one time and let some slip through the net?

Have you ever promised a customer that you'd do something and then forgot? The ultimate Cardinal Sin!

If you struggle with multitasking then make sure you have what is called **"Clean Focus"** - DON'T jump onto something else until you have fully finished what you're currently working on.

Some people excel at juggling tasks and priorities, others prefer to be focussed. We are all different!

Do not be tempted to compare yourself - well at least how you do it - to others. People are successful at the same thing but in different ways. Some football teams are defensive in nature, others play with flair and style - yet the more cautious team may win the league.

Compare Tiger's swing to Phil Mickleson and Bubba Watson to Rory McIlroy - all totally different, one better at some aspect of the golf game than the others - yet they're all major winners, all at the top of the World Rankings.

There is nothing wrong with being individual - **as long as it works** - as long as you hit your targets and goals.

However!

Should you get into the pattern of avoiding Prospecting and New Business Development because you find dealing with existing customers and Account Management easier, less stressful and more satisfying - or vice versa - you hate dealing with the same old faces and ignore long term customers for the thrill of finding new ones because that's exciting and challenging - then you could be heading for disaster.

You'll be like a golfer who hates bunkers. He can't get out of them - so he begins playing to avoid them. Rather than seek the pin out - the target - he plays wide of the green because he needs to risk coming over a bunker to get to the flag.

That may seem like good course management, good strategy by avoiding trouble but it may have cost him a stroke because he now needs to chip on and then putt - whereas he could have been on the green a shot earlier, if he wasn't so afraid of taking on the bunkers.

That is not Course Management - that is a negative strategy designed to cover up weaknesses. What he should do is go to the practice area and get lessons on how to handle bunker shots, so he can play to his full potential.

Do you have a pattern of avoiding tasks during the day?

If so, ask yourself why?

How can you overcome this weakness that doesn't involve avoiding it? Add it to your Personal Progress Log and set yourself a goal to improve in this area.

To be at the top of the selling game - just as in sports - you need to have no weaknesses or at least be prepared to work on them - to eliminate them. Keep doing what's good and address what could be better.

Finally, identify your daily & weekly patterns. Are you a slave to routines that inhibit your potential? Same customer, on the same day, at the same time? Convinced there's no point calling someone on the phone after 4:00pm on a Friday?

It's imperative that you watch out for and eliminate these self-limiting and often negative thoughts and beliefs. They will not help you succeed. They will only hold you back.

American psychiatrist Daniel G. Amen has named these limiting thoughts ANTs - Automatic Negative Thoughts.[3] They are the gloomy, downbeat, pessimistic and negative thoughts that appear in your head - they are involuntary and most often surface at the least appropriate time.

It's imperative that you stop them in their tracks before they take over and ruin your life. ANTS are habitual and feast on your weaknesses and low self-esteem. Remember they are nothing more than negative self-talk - so when they occur, challenge them, reframe them. Programme yourself to get the best out of every situation, even defeat.

There's never a time when you don't learn something.

Many a sportsperson has admitted they have learned more from a defeat than they have from winning.

If your pattern is one of limiting thoughts and behaviours remember what we spoke about earlier; E+R=O. Change your reaction or response and you will alter the outcome.

Concentration

All top sportspeople have the ability to concentrate when it matters most.

Staying in the moment and knowing your game plan is part of that process. Being aware of what's happening next, why and how you are going to do it, all helps focus the mind when it matters most.

Now, in some sports it's harder to concentrate than in others. You cannot stay focussed constantly for 4 hours during a round of golf - you have to be able to switch it on and off and back on gain when it matters and that's the same when selling.

You need to be able to turn on the tap when it's required and a technique sportspeople use to achieve this is to have a **Trigger** that tells them to get into focus.

You may have heard of a pre-shot routine - it's something most professional golfers go through prior to hitting their shot. Its purpose is to get them **zoned into** doing things right, stay in control and avoid thinking about pressure and what the shot means - we will look at this in relation to selling in the next chapter called "Staying in the Zone". However, the whole process begins when the golfer gives his mind a signal to say "let's go" - "focus" - "it's pre-shot routine time" and it's *that* signal that tells him to **concentrate**!

But what is the signal?

It is in fact, anything the golfer wants it to be.

For some, the signal to concentrate and get into their pre-shot routine mode is taking the Driver head cover off on the tee. At other times it may be removing the putter cover, or when discussions with the caddie about distance and target is finished and the caddie says "OK lets go" - the Pro's been given his verbal signal to concentrate.

These signals just don't happen by chance - they are chosen deliberately, they're selected to mean something significant to the player. In Psychology terms these signals are often referred to as **anchors**. They hold a particular thought or frame of mind in place.

Earlier on we looked at the powerful effect of anchors in Chapter 1 when I described the effect of the song coming through on the radio. That was an example of an auditory anchor. The song will illicit those same feelings in you time and time again.

Did you ask for it to happen? Did you want to change your mood at that precise moment? No - but it did. And that's the power of anchors. And the good news is you can set them up deliberately as well as have them happen to you by chance.

When the golfer touches his Driver or removes the putter cover, when his caddie says, "let's go" - they are signals to concentrate and enter the zone and they help the golfer play to his best. They are the anchors that hold his game together.

In sales you will also find anchors - both negative and positive.

Let's begin by analysing a negative sales situation and how you may overcome it.

If you don't like lifting the phone to make appointments - you've created a negative anchor - the phone means rejection and pain, so you want to avoid it. That is human nature. But you have to make phone calls its part of your job. So how do you go about breaking this negative anchor? The answer is you engage your *logical* mind.

The negative feeling is an automatic reaction. A programmed reaction created by months, even years of being told - "no thanks" when you dial. It's simply your subconscious mind trying to protect you from hurt and pain.

Your thoughts over the years have programmed it to believe making cold calls on the phone hurts!

As we looked at in chapter one, the subconscious mind does not judge, it simply stores and reacts to what it has in its memory banks.

Think of your mind as though it is an iceberg - only about 10% is above the water - that's your conscious mind. Logical. Critical. Factual.

The rest - 90% - is below the water and that's your subconscious mind. The holder of your memories, instincts, emotions, feelings and beliefs - and anchors tap right into this part of the mind.

So if you want to break a negative anchor - like fearing the phone - the key is to get factual not emotional!

Analyse your batting average on the phone. How many calls does it take to speak to how many people - to get how many appointments? 50 calls. 10 connections. 3 appointments?

Assuming you're a confident salesperson, then that's your stats. Perhaps you could brush up on what your opening line is and get 15 connections and so 5 appointments - whatever! But 100% success is probably not realistic. So get factual to combat emotion. What are your colleague's stats? Get info to help your logical mind fight your negative anchors.

Become rational. Prospects are not rejecting you; they are rejecting your proposal. They haven't met you yet, so how can they not like you! Why take it personally?

If lifting the phone hurts, remember it's only your ego that's taking a beating. How would you cope with being a boxer who doesn't like being punched? I'm sure none enjoy it but they recognise its part of the game. If they go in the ring they're going to get hit no matter how good they are.

You've heard the expression "boxing clever" but what do you think it means?

Boxing clever to a salesperson is doing what you can not to get dragged into negative, emotional situations where your subconscious takes over and ANT's crawl all over you!

Defeat negative emotions by the use of logic. Focus on the facts and your conscious mind will help combat the negative thoughts.

So what about Positive Anchors?

You may want to encourage your instinctive emotional feelings when they work for you, when they are positive and productive. That's what's happening in the golf examples I gave earlier. The logical, factual mind that will focus on what the shot means; $1m, the Open Championship and 10 years qualification exemption on the tour - is shoved aside and replaced by the subconscious following a well-rehearsed pattern, the pre-shot routine, designed to keep players in the moment and pressures away - the first part of which is switching on your concentration.

This is something you should get into the habit of doing when selling too. Tell your mind, every time you close the boot or touch the fob to lock the car and hear the "beep, beep" - tell your mind - "Show time" - "Game on" and get the sense of confidence rising.

As mentioned before, think about past successes as you walk into reception. Keep doing this - associate the positive feeling of past successes with the "beep beep" and trigger phrases like "Let's go" and it will eventually become sub-conscious - in other words it will become **habit** and you will have created an anchor to set you up for the perfect call.

Remember, 90% of what we do on a daily basis is habit, so programme positive ones.

To help you get into the way of setting anchors, let's create one right now. You can also think of the following when using your trigger phrases or doing the trigger action such as hitting the fob, closing the boot or tapping your brief case:

If it's safe to do so, what I'd like you to do is very gently and lightly, stroke one of the knuckles on your left hand as you read the following out loud.

I have a Mind-set that makes me feel prepared and ready to sell:

I know being prepared will encourage my confidence to grow.

When I feel fully prepared, I feel ready to sell.

When I feel ready to sell, I am relaxed and in control - both of which adds to my confidence.

I feel confident in my skills:

Confidence is the key to my success and the main objective of my mental preparation.

I've reviewed my game plan and I'm focussed on the areas I wish to address during the call.

I have pride and confidence in my abilities.

I am confident because I have practiced, because of my previous successes and customers' trust in me.

OK, you can stop stroking your knuckle now and just let those thoughts sink in for a moment. Take note of the feelings you're experiencing as you do so.

Is there a tingle in your knuckle, perhaps a flutter in your heart?

Is your confidence raised? Do you feel better? Stronger?

Repeat the exercise above and feel free to use any words or phrases that suit your own style. Try it a few times. Gently stroking the chosen knuckle on your left hand.

I appreciate some of you may feel a little embarrassed saying those phrases out loud. Well if that describes you, it goes to show how little of your self-talk is positive. All those thousands of words you say to yourself every day and you get embarrassed by saying something good about yourself! How programmed are you to be one of those who's internal dialog is 80% negative?

Time for a change don't you think?

Have you ever heard Usain Bolt talk himself down? Or Mohammed Ali at his peak? No chance.

The same principles apply no matter where you look; in sport, industry, commerce or the arts; self-belief produces winners and the first person that has to "believe" is you.

So make your self-talk a positive, encouraging, motivational dialog instead of a negative one and anchor the feelings as you do.

When you get used to creating anchors, they can be powerful triggers to keep you confident and in the zone when selling or presenting.

For example, if during a call things are getting a little tough - you can gently touch the same knuckle to kick in those confident feelings just when you need it. No one will notice. It's your little confidence booster secret.

Still don't believe?

Well the next time you watch a round of golf on TV, take note of the routines, idiosyncrasies and actions golfers make - all different but all with one aim in mind - getting focussed on playing the shot.

For the future and to stack the anchor and make it stronger, read this part over and over and repeat the action of stroking your knuckle.

Any time you get a success, a compliment, a sale - add them all into the mix by gently touching your anchor knuckle as you think about the success and how it makes you feel.

Keep stacking your anchors. Use as many items and situations as you can as sources of positive inspiration and get your subconscious mind working for you automatically rather than against you.

Think positively when you lock the car. Associate the "beep-beep" or door "click" with success.

Reflections on Mental Skill Number 4:

Break down your sales process into its various stages.

What are the objectives for each stage?

Note down any patterns you work to - develop good ones and work to eliminate bad ones.

Remember to create positive anchors.

Mental Skill Number 5:

Staying in the Zone and Selling with Confidence

Mental Skill Number 5:

Staying in the Zone and Selling with Confidence

One of the most important mental skills in sports is the ability of an athlete to focus on the present (the here and now).

For example, in golf this requires a player to concentrate on the mental processes that allow him to execute a swing. This can be different for each player and as I mentioned in the last chapter they form part of what is known as the pre-shot routine. These processes involve the thoughts, images, feelings, targets, etc. that should fully occupy the golfer's mind during shot execution.

The key principle behind this is; that focussing on the execution of each shot helps the player avoid thinking about results or match outcomes - as too much focus on these can lead to tension, anxiety and sometimes doubt - which in turn may well ruin their round.

Now let's think about that for a moment: the point of having a pre-shot routine is to avoid thinking about the outcome - in other words thinking about what the shot means - because it's outcome thoughts that lead to tension, anxiety and perhaps doubt.

Why does a professional, talented golfer miss a three foot putt for the Open Championship? Yes, its pressure. Yes, its nerves. But the pressure and nerves appear because he's thinking of what the three foot putt means - $1m, the Open Championship and 10 years qualification exemption on the tour - he's focussing on the *outcome* of the shot rather than focussing on the *process* of playing the shot.

How often does the outcome of the overall sales call - the order - come into your mind?

What about being behind on your sales targets? Does this make you focus too much on the outcome of the call and not enough on the process of making the sale? This can lead you to jump too quickly to try and close and perhaps come across as desperate or even a little aggressive.

That's why earlier this book we looked at understanding your sales process thoroughly. Not every call to a prospect or customer will have the same objective, especially if a sale traditionally takes 8 months to a year to complete.

The game plan will help keep you on track as to what you should be doing - what your objectives should be - on each and every call.

In this respect - Selling is the same as Sports.

In Golf: Players focus on the process of playing their shot - they create a routine that keeps them concentrating on the process - get this right and they know the outcome will take care of itself (most of the time) but definitely more frequently than if they focus on "I need this putt to make the cut" or

"Only two more pars to win the tournament" - those thoughts generate too much unwanted pressure.

In Sales: Focus on your sales process - get a routine that identifies the clear objectives for each and every call; one that moves you towards the sale one meeting at a time. Know what your outcome is for that particular call and focus on the process of achieving it. Get this right on each and every call and at the very least you'll still be standing when the order is on the table, months down the line.

If the sale is a big one and you're out of your comfort zone - having a process to work to is even more important because *then* the pressure *will* be on and if you focus on the outcome you may well get uptight and probably make mistakes.

For example, if it's customary for potential customers to question your price and when you deal with the objection, some end up buying and some don't - this can be said to be part of your *normal* sales process. Receiving price objections is par for the course and you accept that - as well as accepting some will not buy at the price you're selling at.

But suddenly you're vying for an order that's 10 to 20 times larger than normal or trying to win business from a large prospect, who could buy truckloads of your product in the future. Now the same objection, "you're too expensive" - can grow arms and legs.

But why does this happen?

Answer: Because you're doing what poor sportspeople do - you're focusing on the **Outcome**. Your mind is saying "If I don't get this right, I'll lose the order!" the same as a golfer saying to themselves "only one more par to win the tournament".

A lot can happen between the tee and green, especially if outcome thoughts lead to nerves and anxiety. That's how sportspeople blow it when they look odds on to win.

DON'T DO THAT! DON'T' ENTERTAIN OUTCOME THOUGHTS!

Follow your sales process and stay focussed on where you're at in the sale.

If they object to your pricing, go through your routine of handling the objection. If you're calm and confident - that will come across. If you flap due to the size of the order - that will come across too and an experienced buyer will smell blood! Don't let the size of the outcome affect the way you deal with the objection. Play it the same way as though it was a normal order.

Am I saying you'll win without discounting? Of course I can't guarantee that but what I can guarantee is that if you flap and panic there is a strong possibility you will lose the order or at least give away more discount than you would like, to win it.

However, if - and I'll say it again *IF* - you have prepared your game plan, factored in the differences because of the size of sale it is (just as golfers prep differently for links courses to parkland or high altitude) - you should be prepared and still be sticking to your process and let your well-honed selling skills take over.

Perhaps you could have discussed volume and prices with your Sales Director prior to the call, or even have him or her with you in the call if it's that important.

Success lies in preparation and then sticking to your processes and routines.

If you follow the ideas and processes given to you in this book - ideas and processes used successfully by professional sportsmen and women competing at the highest level - they *will* stand you in good stead because you will exude confidence and control and that plays a big part in both the psychology of competition *and* selling.

Now what if your sales process is much shorter; you're expected to Close the Sale on each and every call?

Then what we've discussed is all the more important: Having your game plan, knowing your sales process and strategy, having the answers to objections, knowing your products and service's benefits, your market, your competition etc. It all needs to be in there. Learned! So you can focus on the process of selling and closing but now it happens every call - rather than being spread throughout a year or longer.

When it comes to selling, there is no difference in the idea of working a process - it's just the duration.

The World Golf Match Play events are over 18 holes - 1 round. You win or you're out! Whereas most competitions are over 72 holes & 4 days, a longer duration but the players still have pre-shot routines, concentration triggers and game plans whether it's for 1 day or 4 days. They have to - else they will definitely lose!

Staying in the Zone

Now the title of this session includes the words - Staying in the Zone. So what is the Zone!

In Golf - Playing in the Zone is simply a way of explaining when everything falls into place and the game just seems to happen.

A new player will notice this feeling sooner than an experienced player because as players progress their abilities in the game - their aims and objectives change. I wouldn't personally think of myself being "in the zone" just because I had 2 pars back to back for instance - it would probably register when I had played 5 or 6 holes without dropping a shot.

And it's the same scenario in sales.

A new sales person, who gets three orders in a row in one day - will feel elated whereas the old head, who's read it, seen it and got the tee shirt, may take longer to get the sensation - as they've had many a good day.

So the "Zone", is really a way of describing a more or less perfect game, round or selling day when it all came together.

But is an event like this just a fluke?

Well, to be honest it can be. We all can experience an exceptional day. But I would counteract this by saying there is a difference to a quality day just happening to us by chance to one that's happened by design and one that happens time and time again.

Everything you have covered within these pages is conceived to bring results to you by design - not by chance! And there are people out there doing it every day, all benefiting from these techniques.

Even those who don't subscribe to the "Psychology" side of things - when analysed - are actually putting into practice Game Plans and Strategies for Selling and following Processes when in front of customers.

So how do you create a **State of Mind** that you can rely on when selling, one that'll keep you in the Zone?

1. You need to involve as many of the key mental skills covered here as you can. That will mean creating a routine that sets you up for your selling day.

2. You must stay in the present moment. Focus on the Process of selling not the Outcome.

3. You cannot be afraid to make mistakes. Sell freely and with confidence. Remember, doing what you've always done will get you what you've always got.

4. You have to quickly brush off distractions and need to be able to cope with the emotions and excitement of selling well - as well as handing setbacks.

5. To achieve the "Zone", you will need to prepare your mind prior to the day beginning and throughout the day, sell focussing on your process and have the discipline and patience to keep a good day going.

But a word of warning - If you succeed in all of the above, you will undoubtedly be *out* of your comfort zone and find yourself battling outcome thoughts and targets throughout the day because you will be becoming more successful as you get better and better at these mental skills.

This in turn leads to focussing on the rewards of success - the outcome - "Just one more order to be top of the table" or "12 more cases to hit the over-rider bonus."

If this happens, get back into "process mode" and save the success thoughts and self-congratulations for later at home!

Stay focussed and in your process. Too many sportspeople have had victory snatched away from them because they let their mind wander to outcome thoughts - seeing themselves lifting the trophy before it's actually won. Don't make this mistake when the finishing line is in sight!

Everyone is prone to letting their mind drift. 100% concentration 100% of the time is impossible but being able to switch into process mode when required is a must.

So enjoy the party in your heart as you drive along to the next call. But be ready to use your triggers to signal "**concentrate**" and be up for the next call in full process mode, leaving your outcome thoughts back in the car or at home.

The more you practice this - the better you become - the greater the chances you have of being successful and with success comes confidence and that's what we'll look at next.

Selling with Confidence

No matter what part of the selling game we look at, when we speak about confidence in sales terms we are meaning **self-confidence**.

It's only you who can make the sale happen, it's you who feels apprehensive about using the phone to make an Appointment or handling Price Objections or Closing the Sale - everything in Sales is all about your own self-confidence.

That confidence is gained from a background of past performances; selling well, winning orders or beating personal best targets and how well you do during planning and preparation. So it's important that you mentally log these successes.

So here are some strategies to help you take note of and log the successes you will have - to help build your confidence:

Confidence Strategy number 1: Anchoring

Remember the good days. Remember your successes. Replay them over and over. Look forward to selling to certain customers or industry sectors where you've been successful.

From now on deliberately anchor good days and good feelings as discussed previously.

Stack the anchor and invoke it when you need a boost.

Confidence Strategy number 2: Externalise Errors

Externalise Errors, what does this mean?

How often have you seen a professional golfer, after they have failed to#execute a shot properly, glare at their caddie? It happens all the time. The Pro is externalising their mistake. It couldn't possibly be that they miss-hit the shot or took the wrong line! No, it was their caddie's fault and that's that!

Unfair? - Not at all!

The Pro knows he has enough on his plate staying ahead of his fellow competitors without helping them by sabotaging his own confidence and focus by using destructive self-talk about his shot making.

No, the bad shot was down to the caddie, mud on the ball, bad lie, spike marks on the green etc.

In this relationship, the Caddie understands this! Part of his job is to be the Agony Aunt and verbal punch bag during the round. After all he gets paid for it!

Use this technique when you make a mistake. Externalise the error. It's truly liberating. Your confidence will benefit from it.

But be honest with yourself too. If a player did mishit a particular shot a few times during the round, he will work on it on the range afterwards. The externalising is a temporary technique so he doesn't pull his confidence down during the round.

And so it should be with you when selling.

Don't get down on yourself because you are struggling to close sales that day. Wait until you get home or after your last call and reflect on why? What did you do differently? Why did 3 customers who were set to buy, decide against it.

Analyse it logically, unemotionally. No room for negative anchors please! And then be honest enough to go and practice or work on your technique if you feel that was the cause of the failure. Only you will know.

But keep your head up during the day. Don't get dispirited when you are in the game.

Confidence Strategy number 3: Positive Self Talk

Another Confidence Strategy is to keep your confidence high by saying the right things to yourself.

Do you get a lift when someone says "Well done" or "You've really helped me there"?

Well why not do it for yourself - you curse at yourself often enough and call yourself every name under the sun when you make a mistake, so why not turn this around and be nice to yourself for a change during the day?

If you stop being negative about yourself and your lot, at the very least, you will stop dragging yourself down.

Every person carries on an internal dialogue as we've alluded to throughout this book. Your self-talk can be positive: "I will sell well today" - or negative - "I hope I don't screw up and lose that order."

The ideal goal for a salesperson is to maintain positive self-talk before, during **and** after your selling day.

So, develop a list of positive statements that will help you sell well, such as:

"Just relax, you're the best Closer."

"Calm and relaxed - you love the challenge of making appointments - let's get this one nailed, he's a great prospect.

"Clear Buying signal! This is what you do it for - Relax and Close it."

Make sure your statements suit your own language and above all else use them to keep your confidence high.

When you're in the heat of the battle, no one is going to help you feel confident. You must be self-reliant and bolster your own confidence.

Confidence Strategy number 4: Be Pro-active about your Confidence

Many Salespeople don't take full responsibility for their own confidence; they unintentionally wait until their day begins before they make a judgment about how confident they should feel. They wait to see how the first few calls go, hoping for positive results, to give the green light that they should be confident on that particular day.

Don't allow your confidence to wait for a positive start to the day before kicking into action.

Your confidence comes from years of study, knowledge, practice and repetition, not just the last few minutes selling.

So take control and be pro-active:

Prior to selling, go back in your mind's eye and review the last time you sold well.

Experience yourself reliving the sale in which you had complete confidence.

Did you feel unbeatable?

Feel the confidence lift your chest and energise your mind.

Anchor the feelings - put them on tap for when you need them.

Before going into visit a prospect you should recall the feelings and thoughts associated with confidence and project them into the up and coming call.

Visualize yourself performing with high levels of confidence and let those feelings sink into your subconscious.

Your past success is what gives you the belief that you can do it today. Nothing can prevent you from drawing on past successes as a confidence booster for the current day.

Confidence Strategy number 5: Patience and Planning

The best Salespeople don't leave confidence to chance, they prepare to sell and anticipate situations arising. They develop a game plan or strategy; as discussed previously.

Being prepared increases your confidence. Being prepared for the type of customer, the type of industry or simply being prepared for the weather, all influence your confidence to sell on a given day.

Do you become unsettled by unanticipated events that happen during the day? If so, you need to consider them before hand and anticipate how you will cope should they happen - so they will not sap your confidence!

Some common challenges to anticipate during a day's selling could be: difficult weather conditions, psych-out attempts from customers, no shows - where customers aren't there, slow traffic, bad luck and even unexpected equipment problems such as breaking your demonstrator or sample - what would you do?

Developing what we could refer to as a "**coping strategy**" - what you would do and how you would tackle these problems should they arise during the day - will help you carry on with focus, confidence and composure.

So take time to consider events that may occur and work out mentally, in advance, what you will do should they happen - that way they're not so distracting and you can remain in charge of what's going on.

Patience

In Sales, as in Sport, **Patience** is also closely linked to confidence and is probably the most highly sought after commodity when things are not going according to plan.

If the opening calls are bad or you can't seem to get the sale you require to ensure you make target, impatience creeps in, bringing with it negative emotions and almost guaranteed bad results.

Impatience occurs when a salesperson is not performing up to his or her own expectations and can immediately sap confidence.

Do you think top goal scorers stop shooting if they miss a couple of chances early on in the game? I don't think so! The misses simply reinforce their belief that the next one's going in. They know it's the law of averages. The chance they've missed simply means that the next goal they're going to score is coming nearer.

To repeat what was said in chapter one, the top professional golfers in the world only win 10 to 20% of the time they play. So do they get angry and down when it's not going well? Some have and then instantly regretted it because the red mist ultimately has cost them not just the tournament but the chance of coming second or third as they end up way down the leader board, picking up a cheque that barely covers their expenses.

Sportsmen and women who have patience remain confident knowing that their performance, although not satisfactory right now, will get better **and Salespeople can learn from that**.

Look upon patience as a form of confidence about the future - a quiet self-assurance that things will get better or improve with time - if you wait for it and keep visualising it happening.

Once again, that is why goals are important because they keep you on the right track even when you're feeling down or agitated. They give you the reason to get back into focus and stop feeling sorry for yourself.

So keep believing. Your time will come. You're too skilful and professional for the slump to continue for long.

Salespeople with a fragile state of confidence have trouble "waiting" for their performance to improve, so practice your confidence strategies, this will help you become patient; which in turn will feed your confidence - it's a simple self-fulfilling process.

Reflections on Mental Skill Number 5:

Develop a plan to help you stay in the Zone each day.

Consider things that could go wrong and develop coping strategies to keep you focussed should they happen.

Determine which Confidence strategies suit you best.

List your answers below:

Mental Skill Number 6:

Dealing with Setbacks

Mental Skill Number 6:
Dealing with Setbacks

When your day is over and you've sold well, recall the good points and positive outcomes and anchor them as discussed previously, this will stack your positive anchors and aid your selling next time around.

This is a routine I encourage you to develop because if you do, you'll see your confidence and self-belief increase dramatically. Don't let good feelings go. Grab them. Anchor them. Use them.

But what do you do if things didn't go according to plan?

With practice you will eventually have enough confidence and inner mental strength to combat poor days when they happen and get your selling back on track with ease. Just look at how a top player such as Tiger Woods has bounced back from a career threatening incident and is now back to being world number one.

Solid metal strength is achievable and you'll have the required mental skills well-honed soon.

But in the meantime, if you have struggled throughout your day to get focussed on the process of selling and have constantly wandered towards outcome thoughts or even external thoughts (such as other work related issues or problems at home) - you have to accept that your mind was simply not there today - you were just too distracted for your focus and routines to work.

And this happens, even to the best of Sportsmen and Women as well as Salespeople.

In this event, simply let the bad day go. There's no point having a Post Mortem on a day that was dead to begin with. And despite all of the knowledge you will have accumulated developing your Inner Sales Coach - you will have such days.

How often have you seen a football team, odds on to win, put in a stinker of a performance? Sometimes it's just not going to happen. It's not your day.

Remember, your mind is a very powerful yet subtle thing and since we are talking about selling at what could be called a subconscious level - when you focus on the process of selling and use imagery, sounds, feelings etc. - if your subconscious is preoccupied with other matters you won't overcome it - it's just too powerful.

In this event, you'll perhaps find yourself reverting back to mechanical, outcome oriented selling and will no doubt struggle compared to recent days, when things have been so much better.

So, if this scenario happens to you - accept it during the day and let it go afterwards. Do nothing to reinforce negative anchors. Your disaster of a day was nothing to do with your ability to sell. Let it go. You don't become a poor salesperson overnight.

But what about situations where a good day tapered out?

A day where you lost focus and couldn't get it back?

What about these types of days where you had it and lost it?

It's understandable when an unexpected loss of a sale leads to negative feelings. Salespeople report emotions such as anger, mild depression, frustration, or self-doubt regarding their ability when things go wrong.

So what can you do when faced with such situations?

Well, here are some suggestions:

View the poor performance as a lesson learned.

After a poor performance or loss of a sale, you may initially feel disappointed. However, a poor performance or a loss can teach you a valuable lesson. Wait until a sensible time span has passed (not in the car straight afterwards) and review, dispassionately where things went wrong.

Look at your routines, your processes. What went wrong? Something did.

Did you begin the afternoon by having outcome thoughts and went into a call after a half-hearted attempt at getting into focus? Were you still stewing over *that* call, when you entered your next one?

Be honest with yourself. The fault lies in a breakdown of the process and your pre-call routines. Identify it and work on it, making sure it doesn't happen again.

If you flopped because of an obvious flaw in your skills - then get it seen to.

I know these processes can improve a salesperson's ability when they initially adopt them with their current level of "technical" skills but if you're struggling with a part of your selling skills over and over again (handling objections, appointment making, closing the sale - whatever) get help, else you will fear them coming up and be creating negative anchors.

Perhaps you need some training to help you or coaching from your Sales Manager or external source? But get it sorted!

Set yourself a goal to have it looked at and remember to make the goal SMART.

So keep a sense of perspective when you review a poor performance day - if it's your fault address it. If not - let it go!

We all have bad days.

When you analyse and accept what went wrong you also stop looking to blame someone else for your failures. Being 100% responsible for your actions is essential for success in sport and in business.

Too many people look for excuses for their let-downs. Don't be one of them.

If a sale hasn't turned out as you had planned, ask yourself searching process oriented questions such as:

- What did I do/not do to create that outcome?

- What was I thinking?

- Where was my process?

- What did I miss out?

- What did I say or not say?

And most importantly,

- What do I need to do differently next time to get the result I want?

Every outcome is a learning experience and as I've stated before, you'll always learn more from failure than you will success, especially things about your character.

Remember nothing ever "just happens to you".

When we're focussed and think positively about our goals, plans and objectives we attract things to us.

When we think negatively, the same happens.

The reticular activator system doesn't differentiate. It brings what we focus on. We reap what we sow.

So learn to see the signals for the future so the let-down won't happen again. Listen to your inner mind.

Identify aspects of your performance that are controllable.

Effort and mental preparation are factors that are controllable by you, while factors such as the financial ability of your prospects to pay; weather conditions or poor sales environment in a recession or declining market are things that you cannot necessarily control.

So, when examining the reasons for a poor performance or an unexpected loss of a sale, focus your attention on the factors that *are* controllable by you. Identify where it went wrong and work at eliminating the causes next time by staying focussed on your routines.

And finish your review session by re-enforcing the positive aspects of what you have achieved.

Even if the day was a complete loss - there will have been things you did right - bring them to mind.

Focus on **them**.

Re-affirm the positive nature of addressing the areas where you need to improve - "I'm looking forward to the coaching session and seeing how the boss does it / views it" or "I can't wait for the up and coming sales training"

Programme your mind to focus on the positives in everything and it will eventually become habitual and you will be a happier, more skilful, more successful salesperson.

Reflections on Mental Skill Number 6:

Clearly identify what aspects of the Sales Process are under your direct Control.

What backup plan can you use to retrieve a situation should it go wrong?

List them down here:

Performance Excellence

Performance Excellence

So that's the key mental skills as used by professional sportsmen and women throughout the planet adapted to suit a sales environment:

Working on your Attitude and Self-Talk; Understanding Self-Motivation; Managing Anxiety, Stress and Emotions; Knowing your Game Plan and Developing Peak Concentration; Knowing how to Stay in the Zone and Being able to Deal with Setbacks.

Each one is an important mental skill in their own right but together they're a powerful set of Mental Tools that will help you reach Performance Excellence in Sales and in any other area of life that you chose to apply them to.

However, unless you practice them and apply them, they will simply be words on a page; so to finish off I'm going to Challenge you to strive for genuine Performance Excellence!

I challenge you to create a plan - **starting right now** - that will ensure these skills become second nature and habitual in your life.

There's no point waiting until tomorrow - it may never come!

As the saying goes:

Carpe Diem – Seize the day.

I want you to take this opportunity right now, juice it, and squeeze it for what it's worth because if you don't, someone else will and they will have the advantage.

Here's my challenge:

What does performance excellence mean to you? Hitting your sales targets, finding more customers than ever before? Being top of the Sales Team? Only *you* know.

But I dare you to go far and beyond your current limits.

I challenge you to view your current sales target not as a "top end" "ultimate" figure to reach but a *minimum* level of performance set by *current* traditional ways of thinking.

I want you to go about blowing that figure out of the water by having your own additional over-rider on it. That could be 10%, 20% even 50 or 100% higher - how confident do you feel? How high do you dare go?

In other words, how are you going to prove to yourself (no one else) that you have attained **performance excellence**?

If you're in shock at my suggestion, please don't dismiss the challenge too quickly - as you may automatically do. You know that old instant negative self-talk that's now happening or all those ANTS's running about in your head!

Stop and think for a moment . . .

Sure, if you keep doing what you've been doing, you'll get what you've always got and what is that? Normally hitting 80 to 90% of target? Occasionally 100%?

Whatever you've achieved up until now has been done using current methods of working and current levels of thinking. But now you have the tools to burst right out of that self-limiting belief system.

If you're harbour doubts about the challenge - you only think you can't do it because it's not been done before - by you!

Let me give you a couple of examples regarding self-limiting beliefs:

We live in the twenty first century; everyone knows what power tools are for. We're not surprised by what they can do.

However, if I went back to the early 18th Century and went into a forest and met some lumberjacks and asked them how many trees they could cut down and chop up per day, what would they say? 1 or 2? Perhaps a few more? Who knows?

But if I stood with a smile on my face and said I could clear 10 times what they were doing in half a day, they'd laugh at me - because their current view of the world says they can only do one or two. However, once they saw my chainsaw in action - they'd want one and believe it possible too.

Not too long ago it was a widely held belief that man could never run a mile in under four minutes. Some even believed the heart would burst running at such speed for so long.

That "belief" was debunked on 6th May 1954 when Roger Bannister proved all the sceptics wrong when he crossed the finish line in 3 min 59.4 sec (remember the smallest of margins count).

The taboo was broken.

But the interesting thing is; once Bannister did it, once he showed the world it could be done, others quickly followed. The result was that Bannister's time was beaten only 46 days later - this time in 3mins 58 secs.

Think about that: a feat that had never been accomplished before due to fear and lack of self-belief within those attempting it - was re-written and beaten in a few days.

The rest *now* believed, because they'd seen it done.

By the end of 1957 16 runners had broken the four minute mile and in the last 50 years the record has been lowered many times - it now stands at 3min 43.13 sec.

And it gets better . . . Want to discover true self-belief and performance excellence?

In 1997, Daniel Komen of Kenya ran 2 miles - yes 2 miles - in less than eight minutes!

Doing what Bannister did **twice over**!

What was seen to be impossible by the current thinking of the time - is now consigned to history by athletes who set no limits on what they can do.

There are many examples of individuals refusing to be held back by current or self-limiting beliefs be it in sport, business or in life. Just look at what athletes were accomplishing at the Paralympics or what Felix Baumgartner achieved in 2012.

They all prove without a doubt that what you can conceive and believe - you can achieve.

But the key is BELIEF.

I challenge *you* to go the extra mile; become obsessed with peak performance in everything you do because even if you fall just short of your challenging goal, you'll still be miles ahead of where you would have been using conventional thinking.

Now think about your Sales targets again. Will you take the challenge?

If it helps and suits your nature, discuss your plans with someone you trust someone who will support you and be there for you when needed.

Sometimes a little bit of pressure - positive stress - can help you dig in and succeed and another friendly, trusted individual can be that source.

View them as your accountability partner - someone who you know will keep asking the awkward questions when you begin to slack.

But if you're the private type of individual, it's OK to keep your plans to yourself - just make sure you have the self-determination to set them and see them through.

Either way is good, as long as you commit to the process.

If performance excellence was easy we'd all do it. But it's not.

An article in USA Today pointed out that the average Olympian trains four hours a day for at least 310 days a year for six years before succeeding. That's dedication to performance excellence.

What if you don't have the time? Or is it really that you don't have the will, the desire to change? You're happy in your comfort zone?

Let's look at time for a moment and one particular pastime of many adults!

According to the Broadcaster's Audience Research Board, UK adults watch more than 30 hours of TV a week - that's in excess of 4 hours per day. In the USA that figure rises to 6 hours per day.

So if you're a typical 40 year old UK resident, you've spent 3½ years watching TV since you were aged 20; and almost 5 years if you're from the USA! Three and a half to five years of your life gone. All that time spent on your backside, vegetating.

These figures for the average adult obviously get worse the older they are but don't despair too much. If this describes you - I'm not suggesting you abandon your favourite soaps altogether. Just use the technology you have at your disposal to plan better; use Catch up TV or record and series link and watch only the things that genuinely interest you - at a time to suit you.

Over the 20 years, if the average Joe had cut back just 1 hour a day and dedicated it to working on their goals and attaining performance excellence - they would have had 303 days - nearly an extra year - available to them to have done something really productive with their lives.

However, that time is gone. You cannot replace it but you can commit to not wasting it ever again.

Get passionate about your goals - Focus on what you want out of life and work at it.

An hour spent each day working on your plan for success instead of being in front of the TV will give you 365 hours over the next 12 months to help you succeed. That's 15 extra days. Now you have 12½ months to the average Joe's 12.

Working this plan will still allow an average 3 hours a day in front of the "live" TV should you wish to do so – it'll still be there for you over 20 hours a week!!

I'll leave you to do the math!

I appreciate not everyone is addicted to TV – but many are. So if it's your time evaporator think about the above suggestion.

If it's not – what is? Think about where your time goes and ask yourself searching questions – what can you do to get more time dedicated to success, goal orientated activities?

So to finish this chapter, may I remind you that if you've came through Develop your Inner Sales Coach in one go, can I suggest you go back to the beginning and work your way through each chapter once more and take on board and implement each learning point.

They work.

They've been proven to work.

And now they're yours to utilize.

Enjoy the challenge. Enjoy the journey. Enjoy your success.

Reflections Performance Excellence:

What targets are you going take on and by when?

List them below and then break them down into manageable chunks.

Remember SMART! Also give time to considering how you are going to do things differently from now on.

How are you going to blast though your self-imposed ceiling?

Practical tips on Keeping Positive when being hit with Objections

Keeping positive is essential when a prospect or customer challenges what you are saying. Not just so they realise you have faith in what you're proposing but so you don't unwittingly erode your own self confidence.

Let's be logical for a moment. It's human nature to doubt. You may be proposing something totally new or suggesting the prospect leave their present supplier with whom they have had an excellent relationship for years - the fact is *any* "change" elicits doubt.

So the key is to be prepared for the "objection" and not fear it. Accept it as part of the sales process. In many ways objections are a good sign - the prospect or customer is still interested, else you would be out the door by now!

So how you react to and handle objections is a critical skill, not just for getting the sale but to keep your self-esteem and positive self-worth intact. The more you accept that objections are a natural part of the sales cycle and the better prepared you are to handle them, the easier you will take them in your stride when they arise and allow them to improve your confidence rather than erode it.

Treat them like hazards on a golf course; bunkers, water and rough. Learn how to play out of them and you'll never fear them, they won't be an issue to you.

So here are some ideas - applied steps - to help you handle the negative side of selling and keep your confidence high.

I will focus on two specific areas; Getting in the Door and dealing with the Price Objection. The day to day objections you get hit with relating to specific features and benefits of your products or services will have to be noted and responses found by yourself, else you will come unstuck every time they arise. And that is something I would strongly encourage you to do.

However, you may well get some inspiration from the responses I list below.

Getting the appointment on the Telephone

It may be part of your selling strategy to find business by cold calling and turning up on the door step. However, more and more businesses will not see salespeople without an appointment - so somewhere, sometime you'll need to call the prospect in advance.

And what will you hear?

Not Interested? I'm too busy? Send me a brochure first? Probably a multitude of variations on these themes.

Remember, most people don't like change and *you* are change!

So what can you do?

First, **be ready for it**.

How many years have you been selling? What objections have you heard? Get answers for them.

If you don't, you'll be like the boxer entering the ring who can't block a punch - no matter how good he is, he's susceptible to being knocked out before he throws a punch himself.

So try these responses or your version of them when trying to get an appointment:

Objection: "Not Interested"

Mr. Prospect I wouldn't expect you to be at this stage, I've not said anything to interest you yet. That's why I'm calling in advance. I don't believe in wasting people's time. All I'm looking for is 10 minutes to see if there's any common ground. If there's not, you can happily throw me out. How about 9:50am next Thursday or Friday morning?

Objection: "I'm too busy"

Mr. Prospect, That's why I'm calling in advance, I don't believe in wasting people's time. It'll only take 10 minutes of your time to see if there's any common ground. If there's not, you can happily throw me out. How about 9:50am next Thursday or Friday morning?

Objection: "Send me the details first and I'll have a look"

Mr. Prospect I'll happily send you through a couple of sheets of info but that won't tell you if it's the right solution for you. All

I'm looking for is 10 minutes of your time to see if there's any fit for you. If there's not, you can happily throw me out. How about 9:50am next Thursday or Friday morning?

You get the point. Acknowledge the objection but then turn it around.

All good salespeople know that they should "fact find" first - you ask questions about the current situation, what does the prospect do at the moment? Are there any issues? etc. etc. You find out information first before you "pitch" - so you can mix and match the suitable benefits to the customer.

So if that's your usual M.O. the prospect will spend the 10 minutes talking about *themselves* - which everyone is happy to do. And the appointment will probably go on much longer.

In all my years selling I've only had one prospect take off his watch and say "go" when I arrived - and he had a smile on his face when he did it.

What you do after the "fact find" phase depends on your sales process - after they've stopped talking do you start selling benefits, introduce an idea and then go away and create a proposal, pitch and close the sale on the day? It all depends on your sales process.

The point of this section is to help you get in the door.

On a final note, making the appointment ten to the hour is not done by chance. You have asked for 10 minutes. If you say you'll be there at 11:00 o'clock the prospect will automatically and totally involuntary assume you'll want an hour of his time and put up resistance.

If you say, 11:30 am, they will assume you want at least ½ an hour and may also object.

You're asking for 10 minutes, so take 10 minutes.

Make your appointments 10 to the hour. You are being honest. If the call goes on longer it's a good sign and it will be done because the prospect is interested - either in telling you more about themselves or asking you about what you do.

People buy people first and people like talking about themselves, their work and their issues.

The 10 minutes you ask for is only the beginning.

Handling Price Objections

Now let's turn our attention to the most common objection of them all - the Price Objection and find ways of dealing with that.

You're too expensive.

How much?

You'll need to sharpen your pencil!

You've heard them all - the price objection comes in all shapes and sizes.

However, the true power behind handling the Price Objection comes from your own confidence in dealing with the situation. It's Psychological. And there are various ways of ensuring you cope with confidence and conviction.

Method 1

Objective: Be aware of why your prices are what they are. And be proud of them!

Draw a graph with an x and y axis and put a dollar, euro or pound sign against the vertical axis.

Now add little boxes starting at the bottom, each one representing a facet of your company that makes up your price.

For example the boxes may represent Raw Materials, R&D, Staffing Cost, Sales & Marketing, Profit etc. etc. You add whatever suits your company's situation.

In the end you will have a graphical picture of what makes up your price.

Now if you have competitors who are cheaper than you, consider why? Perhaps they don't have R&D, they only copy others in the market or perhaps your employment terms and conditions are much better than theirs. That has to be paid for somehow!

The point is, it's highly unlikely they will have the exact same overheads as you *and* be cheaper.

Be proud of your prices.

That's psychological technique No. 1.

Method 2

Objective: Establish the difference.

When a prospect objects to your price find out what he's comparing it to.

If he says, "You're too expensive", you should ask, "By how much?" or "In relation to what?"

You need to know how far out you are.

If your price is 10,000 and you're being compared to something that's 7,000 - the customer is complaining about the 3,000 difference not the 10,000. So you need to know what you're up against. If they won't tell you, method 3 will show you what to do.

However, if you can establish the difference, you then break it down for them:

"OK, so on the face of it we're 3,000 "more expensive" let's look at that, can we?"

"As you know the x,y,z will be in service for 5 years. That's working out at 600 per year more or to put it another way 1.64 per day for the peace of mind of having a 24 hour call out and full service and support for the 60 months. That's 1.64 for service and support you'll not get if you go for the other machine."

It could be the warranty or simple build quality that's better but justify the price difference.

Method 3

Objective: Sell the benefits differentiation.

To a degree this is similar to the above example but it relies on you knowing that the prospect sitting opposite fully understands *and* appreciates that you are a better quality product or service. They are just having difficulty accepting the price.

You don't even need to know what the competition's price is (although it's always nice if you do - especially if the prospect happily tells you, it means they like you!) But even if they just say "you're way too expensive", this technique works.

Draw two bars on a bit of paper, like you see below.

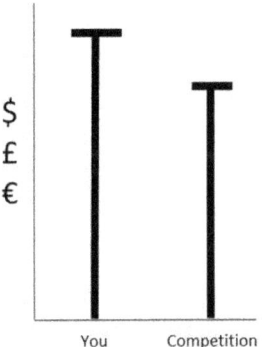

$
£
€

You   Competition

Remember, you must be SURE they know the difference between your offering and the competition's in terms of benefits and features etc.

Now you simply say, "OK, that's us, that's the competition (or company X if you want to name them), who's would you buy if we were the same price?"

Then you shut up!

Chances are (knowing yours is the better product or service), they'll say "Yours" - fully expecting you to match or get near the lower price.

Just smile and nod, look them in the eye and ask, "Why?"

After a moment's silence, the prospect may say something like, "Well . . . you're giving the 24 hour support and back up and your warranty is for 2 years not 12 months . . ." and as they talk to you (giving you all the reasons why your offering is better!!!) you simply smile and nod and when they finish, you say . . .

"Exactly! That's why we're here (point to the graph) and not there (point to the competition's bar). If we didn't offer all those benefits I can tell you our price would be lower than what they're pitching at. It's all those things you mentioned that make us value for money."

As the penny drops in the prospects mind, you could try and close by saying something like, "So will we go ahead and get it organised you're obviously keen on the features of our service."

With a little luck, you'll close the sale but even if they are a trained and seasoned professional buyer and still hold out for a better price, you'll get by without having to discount the full amount or price match - at least retaining a better margin - because you now know they want what you're offering and so do they.

Method 4

Objective: Demonstrate the Return on Investment.

Throughout Europe you see large haulage trucks and heavy goods vehicles that now have a curve and slope on the trailers they pull behind. This is to make them more aerodynamic and fuel efficient because of the cost of diesel.

But these trailers are more expensive to buy than the traditional rectangular box shape - so the sellers have to financially validate the price differentiation and prove it's a worthwhile investment: the slope causes less drag, which equates to fuel efficiency and savings and these savings more than cover the price differentiation.

Now, I'll demonstrate how to do this with a couple examples in a moment but I'd like to say this method works across all sectors and for all products and services. It's used by sales teams from the Engineering Sector, Food and Drink, Electronics, Health & Medical Supplies, Office Supplies and the Service industry to mention just a few.

It's all about demonstrating financially why using your equipment, stocking your products or working with your service makes financial sense.

Think about it, you have spent time - perhaps months - selling the features and benefits of your product or service, now you simply want to demonstrate how and why, what you are proposing makes sense.

You can have an example already prepared or take your customer though it "live" as you create a customized ROI model in front of them or actually incorporate it into your quotation document as well - instead of just listing prices.

Here are two examples so you get the idea.

Example A: Super Industrial Seals Ltd.

	Current Seal	Our Super Seal
Price ($,£ or €)	100.00	900.00
Replacement Per Annum	6	2
Time for replacement	4 hours	30 minutes
Total replacement time PA	24 hours	60 minutes
Seal Costs PA	600.00	1800.00
Labour Costs @ 35.00ph	840.00	35.00
Downtime Costs 150.00ph	3600.00	150.00
(Lost Profit on Production)		
Seal replacement Cost PA	5040.00	1985.00

Total Savings per Production Line of 3055.00 when using the "Super Seal".

Now an example from a totally different industry.

Example B: Fine Foods Ltd.

	Current Profit per shelf	"Our Products" Profit Per shelf
Jars per shelf	48	48
Net Price ($,£ or €)	64.80 (1.35each)	93.60 (1.95each)
Re Stock PA	6	6
Total stock cost PA	388.80	561.60
RRP	777.60 (2.70each)	1123.20 (3.90each)
Profit PA	388.80	561.60

Total improvement in T/O and Profit of over 40% per Shelf when switched to "Our Products"

Even the most seasoned of buyers find it difficult to argue with return on investment demonstrations like that.

The key is to ask the appropriate questions during the Fact Find stage of your sales process. Once you have the data you can produce accurate ROI models.

Look at the two examples given. At face value both companies would get hit with the price objection.

In example A, the seal is 9 times the price of the one currently being used - think of the prospect's immediate reaction to that! Its only when the "whole cost" of staying with the incumbent supplier is taken into account, does the 900 look great value.

Use Return on Investment demonstrations to make you proud and confident of your prices.

Next time, when someone laughs at you being 9 times the price you won't flinch because you expected the punch to come. However, you have the perfect block and counter punch ready and waiting - and with self-esteem and self-confidence intact - you'll power towards your performance excellence goals.

Reflections on Practical Tips:

What methods are you going to adopt to get more appointments and handle objections?

List them below. Learn them.

When will you use them? On who?

Also come up with and list your own answers to common objections you face day to day if you struggle with them. Help yourself stay confident:

Conclusion

If this is your first read straight through, I'm sure your mind will be buzzing with ideas and you'll be desperate to put these methods into practice. And that's one of the best things about learning the inner game of selling, you can practice it anywhere!

You don't need a customer or a prospect to hone many of the skills outlined in this book, it can be done anywhere, anyplace, anytime. Everything you need is in your head.

So read the chapters again and practice what you learn.

Make sure you are confident with the concept of the Key Mental Skills. Once you're happy with what they are - you can focus on putting them into practice to achieve Performance Excellence.

Remember, you must practice them in order to make them second nature. Don't expect things to work on demand if you have never attempted to try them before you use them in earnest.

These are **acquired skills**, that when learned will stand you in good stead for life - not just during a day's selling.

Some of the techniques build on each other, others stand alone.

Some you will use every day, others only occasionally but all need to be understood and learned. Take your time, don't expect miracles but I promise you that the more effort you put in, the faster and easier it will become.

Take confidence from the fact your mind wants to think like this. This is how it works best - that has always been the case; it's just perhaps, it's never been explained to you before on a conscious level. Now, you're being trained to communicate with your own mind in a way it understands.

Enjoy the journey. Your sales results will be all the better for it.

When you Change your Mind - you Change your Life.

Brian McGowan

About the Author

Brian McGowan has been involved in Sales and Marketing since the mid 1980's. With a background and qualifications in engineering, he began his sales career selling specialist building products to architects and specifiers before turning his attention to electronics where he specialised in selling into the larger, corporate marketplace.

By the late 80's the PC revolution was well under way and by aged 27 Brian was Northern European Corporate Sales Manager for a global software house called Aldus, the pioneers of desktop and electronic publishing. By the early 90's by outs and mergers were commonplace across the IT sector and when Adobe took over Aldus Brian moved on to pastures new setting up his own training and development company which he still operates to this day.

Based in Tayside, Scotland, Brian delivers training sessions and courses throughout the UK and abroad demonstrating how Sport Psychology can improve performance across a wide range of business disciplines such as: Sales and Sales Management, Stress Management, Leadership, Communication and Team Cohesion and Motivation. He is a Fellow of the Institute of Sales and Marketing Management.

A qualified Master Hypnotist, NLP Practitioner and holding a Diploma in Sports Psychology, Brian combines the disciplines used widely in the Sports arena and brings them into the workplace. This fresh perspective on Personal and Business development ensures Brian is in great demand from both corporate organizations and private clients as more and more companies and individuals become aware of what these skills have to offer them and their companies.

"The building blocks that make great champions are the same ones that build great organizations and increase personal achievement."

Brian is also a Past Captain of his local Golf Club and author of several books including: Develop your Inner Golf Coach and Develop your Inner Putting Coach and is currently working on his first novel.

Other Books by This Author

The Inner Coach Series

Sport

Develop your Inner Coach:

Golf

Putting

Business

Develop your Inner Coach:

Sales

Sales Management

All available on Kindle

Be different at your next event

At your next Sales Meeting, Staff Conference, Away Day, in-house seminar or Club Event, why not experience how Sports Psychology Techniques and Principles can influence and motivate your staff?

Informative, fun and motivational, Brian McGowan explains why **belief** in your Goals, **mental toughness** and **resilience to failure** are absolutely crucial to success, and his presentation cleverly articulates how this links into challenges faced by his audience on a daily basis.

Using tried and tested mental game principles any individual or team can raise their level of performance to gain success previously thought unachievable. Brian gives a fascinating insight into the world of sports and demonstrates ways that everyone can raise the bar in their own life.

Brian's presentations are both engaging and thought provoking, with content customised to focus on specific needs that are important to you at the time of the event - he leaves delegates motivated to take action.

Services provided to clients include:

Individual & Team Development, Sales Consultancy, Performance Coaching and Keynote Speaking

What are the kinds of issues Brian can help with?

Sales Recruitment, Lack lustre staff, Motivation has died, Talk the Talk but no longer Walk the Walk, Sales are dropping through the floor, Confidence is dying or worse, Team spirit has disappeared, Lost the "Big Picture" vision, Going in the wrong direction, Need a strategy, Don't know why you're losing the deals, Communication is dead, Change management unrest, Company ethos issues. I'll stop because I know you get the picture!

Brian McGowan, MTC Services (Scotland) Ltd

PO Box 6633, Blairgowrie, Perthshire, PH11 8WA

In the UK call: 0845 6800 683

International call: 0044845 6800 683

W: **www.brianmcgowan.co.uk**

One last thing...

If you like what you read and feel it has improved your performance, please feel free to rate **Develop your Inner Coach: Selling** on the site where you purchased it from and also feel free to drop me an email and let me know how you're getting on, you'll find it on my website:

www.brianmcgowan.co.uk

Wishing you all the best and much success in the future,

Brian McGowan

Acknowledgements & Credits

[1] Jack Nicklaus, Legend.

[2] The Success Principles TM, by Jack Canfield. (Harper Collins 2005)

[3] Change Your Brain, Change Your Life, by Daniel G. Amen, M.D. (New York: Three Rivers Press, 1998)

www.ingramcontent.com/pod-product-compliance
Lightning Source LLC
Chambersburg PA
CBHW051806170526
45167CB00005B/1897